# BLACK EMPRESS

Also by and with

# Bobbi Phelps Wolverton

*Flyfishing Always*

*Writes of Passage 2011*

*Behind the Smile:*
During the Glamour years of Aviation

# BLACK EMPRESS

## Rescuing a Puppy from Iran

# BOBBI PHELPS
## WOLVERTON

Published in the United States by Village Concepts, L.L.C.
First Edition.

**Creative Nonfiction Disclaimer:** All names are factual except for the names of the veterinarians. Recollections are to the best of my knowledge. These stories took place in 1967, 1972, and 1973. To aid in the narrative flow, timelines were condensed.

Cover Design by Abraham Tol, Bob Ballard, and Bobbi Phelps Wolverton.

Library of Congress Cataloging-in-Publication Data

1. Wolverton, Barbara Phelps. 2. Wolverton, Bobbi Phelps. 3. Iran. 4. Nepal. 5. India. 6. Author - American. 7. Memoir. 8. Retriever Dog 9. Labrador Retriever.

ISBN 978-0-9970688-0-1

**Visit the author's website at www.booksbybobbi.com.**

Cover photo: Supplied by Shooting Star Photography, N. Logan, Utah. Black Labrador provided by Puppy Steps Training in Northern Utah.

Back cover photo: Bobbi and Bahnoo on Cape Cod in Massachusetts.

*In Memory of*
*Shah Bahnoo Siya:*

*My Black Empress*

# CONTENTS

# CONTENTS (continued)

Iran and Specific Cities

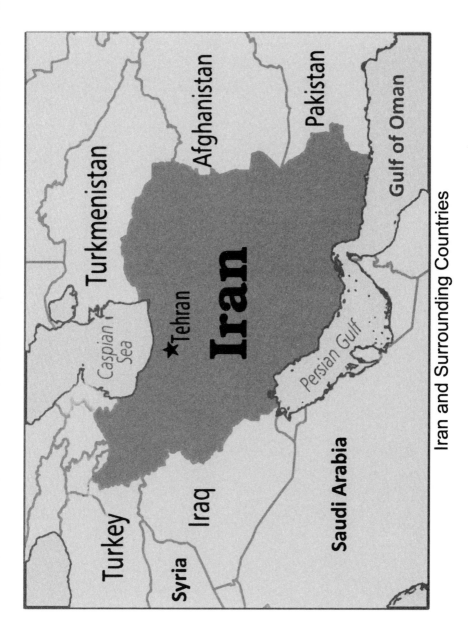

Iran and Surrounding Countries

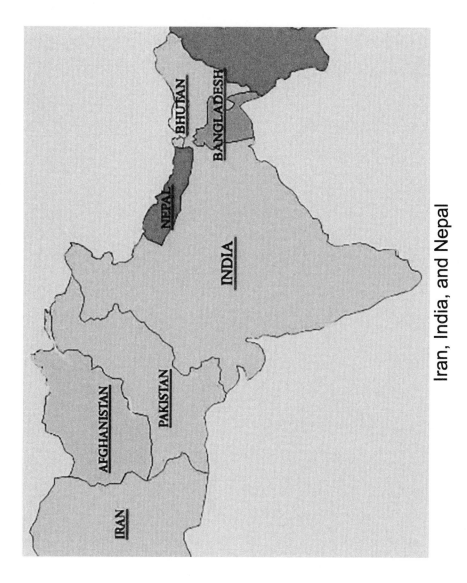

Iran, India, and Nepal

# Chapter One
# The Runt

"Why are you going to kill her?" I asked, clutching the squirming black puppy closer to my chest.

"Why?" I asked, my voice breaking as I repeated the question. "We just spent the last few months trying to save her."

"We don't have pets," answered David Laylin, co-owner of the Iran Safaris Company. He was a slender man in his middle thirties, attractive in a rugged sort of way.

We stood in the tiled entrance hall of the spacious home he shared with his wife, Jill. They had invited Ron and me to stay with them in northern Tehran while my husband worked for the Iranian government, focusing on its oil pollution problems.

"We have only working dogs, and she's not healthy enough to be one," David said as he reached for the scruff of the small Labrador's neck. "She's a sickly runt. There's no way she can retrieve ducks for hours on end," he added. "One of our workers will drown her in the pond."

"No!" I exclaimed, turning my back to him as I smoothed the puppy's soft fur with the tips of my fingers. "Let me send her back to the States."

It was out of character for me to address my host and friend with such audacity, but I loved this little dog and was determined to keep her alive.

Despite my bellbottom jeans, colorful blouse, and long brown hair, I was not a hippie (a dropout or a drug user). Yet I did often question authority and I didn't necessarily follow typical behavioral patterns. Now I was about to become a rebel with a cause — to save this puppy from certain death.

Months earlier when we first arrived at the Laylin home, one of their dogs had just given birth to eight black puppies, all of which were plump, healthy, and active. All, that is, except one. In my arms I held the runt of the litter.

"OK. You can try. But call the embassy first to see if that's even a possibility," said David.

"I asked about the rules when we were at the American Embassy in India," I replied. "She fits the criteria. Now all I have to do is get health papers from your vet."

"Jill and I'll help if that's what you really want," David responded as he crossed his arms. "But if the vet won't give you the proper papers, you know what we'll have to do."

# Chapter Two
# Around the World

As recent university graduates who were both in our late twenties, Ron and I flew to Tehran in October 1972. We had already spent a year of traveling from Africa to Scandinavia and then to the British Isles.

"Let's fly from London to Tehran for a few days," I had suggested while we were still in the States. "I really want to buy a Persian carpet. Do you mind?"

"No, of course not," Ron replied. "I'd like to try fishing in that part of the world. It'd be so different from anything we've done before."

Ron, tall and thin with a manicured mustache, represented numerous fishing tackle companies during our eighteen-month trip around the world. He wrote articles for *Fly*

*Fisherman Magazine* and I took photographs to illustrate his writings.

Before leaving the California bay area on our round-the-world trip, the Iranian Consulate in San Francisco had informed us that this specific outdoor organization, Iran Safaris, produced the best fishing and hunting results in the Middle East. Birds winged their way from Africa to and from the countries bordering the Arctic Ocean. They flew across Iran, one of the countries located on their migrating flyway.

As a former flight attendant for an international airline, we benefited from previously purchased discounted tickets. Each of the tickets for our extensive trip cost only two hundred dollars, 10 percent of the original price.

Iran was under the rule of Shah Mohammad Reza Pahlavi, the king of the country. He had a close relationship with the United States during his thirty-seven-year dictatorship and worked well with our presidents, from Eisenhower to Nixon. His major supporter and personal friend was President Dwight Eisenhower who had ordered the CIA to overthrow the Shah's predecessor.

The Shah was determined to bring Iran into the twentieth century by not requiring the chador, a full-length covering for Muslim women, and by making education more affordable. His family wore Western clothes most of the time and his children attended American universities. Besides studying at Iranian colleges, many wealthy Iranians also sent their children to schools in England, France, and the United States.

Stable military governments in the Middle East during the seventies provided trouble-free holidays for European and American travelers. World War II was over, and the central nations were generally satisfied with their current borders and leaders.

The Islamic Republic of Iran, the country's official name, sat in the middle of a largely dry region of the world. The beauty of the Caspian Sea to the north and the Persian Gulf to the south created a resort-like country that encouraged vacationers to visit. Deserts, rivers, and mountains filled the interior. In the winter one could snow ski near an elegant chalet north of Tehran or swim in the turquoise waters at Bandar Abbas, a city that touched the shores of the southern gulf.

Tehran, however, was a city of contrasts. As the political capital of Iran, it was a chaotic metropolis overcrowded with people and vehicles. Upon our arrival Ron and I checked into the Commodore Hotel, recommended by the incoming cabin crew for its airline discounts. The lofty brick building had an impressive courtyard filled with flowers and fountains, and we were pleasantly surprised by its modern and stylish structure.

We registered at the marble reception desk located in the corner of the entrance hall, an area decorated with Persian carpets and lined with potted palms. Two bellhops lugged backpacks, suitcases, rod and reel cases, wader bags, and photographic equipment to our room on the eleventh floor. From a large window we had a fantastic view of the outskirts of Tehran, the desert, and the gleaming snowcapped mountains in the distance.

Once we had settled into our suite, I changed from my traveling dress to comfortable navy slacks and a beige blouse. Ron stayed in the clothes he had worn on the plane. We then left our hotel to take a cab to the Iran Safaris Company.

"Take only the orange cabs," the hotel concierge instructed. "The other ones are not safe and are probably illegal."

"Let's grab this one," Ron said to me while we stood outside the hotel entrance. He flagged down an orange taxi, and it immediately pulled to the curb.

Ron gave the cab driver the address of the safari company. The concierge had written it in Farsi, the language of Iran, on the hotel's decorative stationery. After nodding his head in agreement, the driver launched us through the downtown streets of Tehran in what turned out to be a ride from hell.

# Chapter Three

# Orange Cabs

As we hurled through the crushing chaos in our orange taxi, we noticed numerous deep chips and extensive scratches on every vehicle we passed. Besides severe dents, many trucks and cars had nonexistent fenders, missing tail lights, and broken headlights.

"Look at these cars," I said. "They're from the fifties and falling apart."

"Yeah," Ron answered. "We left a deluxe hotel for a beat-up jalopy," he added as he wiped cigarette butts off the back door armrest.

From the windows my eyes captured all the various means of transportation in this incredibly active city. Camels and oxen had assorted wares piled high on their backs as they plodded next to sidewalks. Donkeys and horses pulled overstuffed wagons through the main street. And rag-clad men staggered in and out of traffic with their hands clutching wood cart shafts.

A combination of buses, trucks, and motorbikes added to the havoc. With low gasoline prices in this oil-rich country, the road snarled with battered gas-powered vehicles jammed between advancing animals moving their merchandise through the small street spaces.

Bicyclists and pedestrians crowded the walkways, and feral dogs wandered everywhere. Drivers felt exempt from all normal automobile regulations, continuously blasting their horns as they twisted through the smoggy maze of travelers.

The busy main street had four lanes, two going in each direction, plus parking strips, walkways, and open sewer gutters on each side of the road. The drivers, ours included, steered every which way — over the parking spots, on sidewalks, and even across the center line, going against the oncoming lanes of traffic.

"Be careful," I shouted, shocked by his reckless driving. "Slow down!"

The overwhelming noise from blaring horns, yelling pedestrians, and swearing drivers challenged our ears. The taxi did not have air conditioning so our windows were wide open. We would have boiled from the heat if the windows were closed, so we endured the dust and noise instead.

"Saag," the driver shouted repeatedly at other taxis. We learned that it was a derogatory word for "dog" similar to the American word "bitch."

We almost hit an older man wearing baggy clothes and selling lemons from an overflowing hand basket. He maneuvered across the street, inching his way between the stalled cars as our driver blasted the horn at him.

And then it happened.

An entirely different person, a businessman dressed in a dark suit with a white shirt, attempted to cross the street in front of us. He raced from the sidewalk, jumped over the gutter, and darted between the nearby cars.

He didn't make it.

Our orange cab smacked the young man square-on with such force that he smashed onto the windshield, his arms splayed across the front glass. He bounced off, landed on his feet, and shot to the other side, never looking back.

With our eyes and mouths wide open, Ron and I gasped, yelling out in unison, "Watch out!"

The cabdriver, gazing at us in his rearview mirror, roared with laughter. Our shocked reaction seemed funny to him — even hilarious.

Finally with a sigh of relief, we exited the orange cab. "What are the other cabs like if the orange ones are the best?" I commented to no one in particular, shaking my head in disgust.

# Chapter Four
# Iran Safaris

The brightness of the sky above downtown Tehran began to dim. The blue diesel fumes had engulfed the streets, overwhelming the busy city. The loud drone of countless vehicles vanished as soon as we walked through the front doors of the Iran Safaris Company.

There were half a dozen employees crammed into the bustling office, all typing and filing. On the walls were colorful posters of snowcapped mountains towering over fast-flowing streams and framed photographs of smiling hunters posing with their rifles and animal trophies.

We introduced ourselves to the receptionist and waited for her to acknowledge our presence to the company's director. Ron and I stood in front of her desk and examined the black and white photos on the nearby partitions.

"Wait a moment," she said looking up at us from her cluttered desk. "David Laylin is the owner, but he's on the phone."

She soon pushed an intercom button and a tall, thin man opened his office door and walked toward us. We shook hands with Mr. Laylin, an impressive American with a tanned face and sandy brown hair. He wore a light blue, button-down shirt that had been tucked inside his pressed tan slacks. He looked like an Abercrombie & Fitch model who had been plucked from a glossy Madison Avenue magazine.

Hearing our introduction, his wife rose from behind her small wood desk and extended her hand in greeting.

"Welcome to Iran Safaris. I'm Jill Laylin."

A smile came over her lovely face as she thanked us in her clipped British accent for coming to their agency. She had shoulder-length auburn hair that framed her face, emphasizing her soft creamy complexion. She wore a white blouse and a green wool suit with a gold pin on her lapel.

All the other women in the office wore Western-style clothes as well. As Muslims, however, they had arrived and would later depart wearing the chador, an outer garment that covered them from head to toe. Only their faces, hands, and feet were allowed to be shown. Like an overly-long scarf, they clasped the middle of the cloak under their chins and held it tight as they commuted to and from work.

"Come into my office, and call me 'David.' I'd like to show you some photographs," he said. "You'll be surprised at what we offer the outdoorsman."

"That's why we're here," said Ron.

Pictures of hunting and fishing dotted the paneled walls and metal shelves of his impressive office. David waved us to matching seats and settled into a swivel chair behind his dark oak desk. He brought out some Iranian maps, rubbing his hand over the once-folded surface, and pointed to different places he'd like us to see.

Ron and I visited with David for a couple of hours. We learned that he was originally from the horse country in Northern Virginia, near Washington, D.C., and his father had been an international lawyer who had represented Iran at numerous United Nations Security Council meetings.

"My sister," David said "married into a former Iranian royal family and now lives outside Tehran. She persuaded me to move closer. So here I am. What brings you to Iran?"

"I just finished graduate school," Ron said. "I'm here to try fly fishing, maybe even some duck hunting. I write for *Fly Fisherman Magazine*."

Once David knew our agenda involved promoting fly fishing around the world, he wanted Ron to include Iran in his articles and for us to stay longer in Tehran. After our visit he walked us to the front door and invited us to a plush affair that was taking place that very evening.

"Why not join Jill and me tonight at the Royal Tehran Hilton? It's a topnotch hotel. Many famous people have stayed there — movie and sport stars, kings and queens. We can pick you up at six."

He explained the specifics of the night's event as he stood in the office doorway. He added, "The government is hosting the party. We can introduce you to some scientists that specialize in pollution control. Who knows? Maybe they'll want you to work with them for a few months."

Ron and I arrived with Jill and David at the Hilton Hotel wearing the best clothes we had packed. I had put on a knee-length blue chiffon dress, and Ron sported tan trousers, a button-down shirt, and a V-neck sweater. These were the outfits we wore on our extensive journey when we wanted to look our finest. We had one suitcase and one backpack each for eighteen months of traveling. We had packed to conserve space as our traveling luggage also included camera and fishing equipment.

During cocktail time in the grand ballroom, David introduced Ron to Dr. Fred Harrington, a chief scientific advisor to Iran and a friend of the Laylins. Once Fred knew that Ron had received his doctorate from the University of California at Berkeley and had finished his thesis specifically on solving oil pollution problems, he wanted him to join his team.

"Meet some of my associates," Fred said as he presented Ron to a small circle of scientists. A number of them had been educated in the United States and knew Berkeley's reputation as a topnotch chemical engineering school.

"Having you in our group will add to our power and prestige. Plus, we won't have to pay your travel expenses to and from America," Fred stated. "It's a perfect answer for us. How about it? Do you want to join us for a few months?"

Ron tentatively accepted their offer, and said, "I'll ask Bobbi to make sure we can fit it into our travel schedule. Then I'll put together an application so you'll understand my specific capabilities."

He added, "After inspecting Iran's polluted waters, I should be able to come up with a helpful solution. If Bobbi and I agree to your proposal, you'll receive a signed contract in a couple of days."

The four Iranian scientists stood in a semi-circle, smoking cigarettes, and nodded their heads in agreement. They wore dark gray suits with white shirts, looking like any businessman throughout the world. Smiles flowed from one to another as they shook Ron's hand to seal the proposed agreement.

Before long we heard music in the background. The Beatles songs had reached Iran. The sound came from speakers that had been placed in the four corners of the banquet hall. We listened to "Let It Be" and watched several couples dance to the music. The four of us joined the group on the circular parquet floor, swaying to the slow lyrics of the No. 1 record.

As the evening wore down, we waited outside for a valet to retrieve the car. David hummed out loud, pleased with the conversation between Ron and the scientists.

"Would you two like to stay with us if Ron ends up working for the Iranian Government?" David asked. "Bobbi could help with secretarial duties at Iran Safaris. What'd you think?"

"We have a second bedroom suite at the other end of our house. You'll have plenty of privacy, and we'd like your company," Jill added.

Obviously, they had been discussing this topic while dancing for they were in complete agreement. Surprised by this sudden request, Ron said, "That sounds wonderful, but Bobbi and I need to chat."

"What'd you think?" he asked me while standing to the side of the building.

Knowing that our lodging bills would be practically nonexistent and that we would be living with a couple we enjoyed, I ventured, "OK. Let's do it. You know we'll have some super experiences — ones we'd never have if we lived in a hotel."

"Jill and David have lived in Iran for years. They both speak Farsi and like hunting and fishing," Ron said. "What could be better?"

We turned to them, beaming from ear to ear. "Great. We can't believe it," Ron said. "This will be perfect."

"Our driver will collect you tomorrow afternoon at four. That'll give you time to pack and do some sightseeing near the hotel," David stated. "He'll pick up Jill and me afterwards and we'll head for home."

# Chapter Five
# The Grand Bazaar

The first person we met at the Laylin home was Ali Akbar, their cook and all-around assistant. After the introductions, he sauntered back to the kitchen, his sandals flip-flopping as he walked over the copper-colored tiles and Persian carpets.

Their home was a one-story stucco building with a garden, pond, and several outbuildings in an enclosed area surrounded by a ten-foot-high stone and mud wall. Protruding from the crown of the wall, I saw colorful glass, broken shards reflecting in the sunlight. Typical of many third-world countries, these types of walls kept the have-nots from stealing from its wealthier citizens.

Jill showed us to a large room in a wing set apart from the rest of the house. We had a double bed with an attached American-styled bathroom, complete with a shower stall, as well as a porcelain commode and sink. On each side of the bed sat a lamp on top of a nightstand. How lucky we were to have met Jill and David Laylin. Their friendship allowed us to have accommodations we could never have afforded if we had been by ourselves.

Five days before our arrival, their female Labrador retriever, Sable, had given birth to eight puppies. Now they had thirteen dogs living in their compound. The mother and pups stayed in one corner of the kitchen, lying on a blanket. The puppies wriggled next to her in a large wooden box. The top was open so Sable could come and go as she pleased.

Labradors have strong muscular bodies and are known to be wonderful waterfowl retrievers. Their coats are short and dense — perfect for protecting them in icy waters. They are tough and hardy, resilient beyond words. Yet they have gentle spirits and make wonderful family pets. David chose to raise Labradors to aid his clients when they bird hunted with the Iran Safaris Company.

When we settled into the kitchen, Jill knelt down, reached into the box, and picked up the runt of the litter. The pup was exceptionally small in comparison to the rambunctious puppies that jostled around her. She moved slightly, clearly following her instincts.

"Can you see? She's fighting to live," Jill said.

"May I hold her?" I asked, putting out my hand.

Jill offered the weak puppy to me. The small furry body barely covered the palm of my hand. She turned and cradled herself between my fingers. Her eyes had not yet opened.

"What a tiny, tiny puppy," I murmured and softly rubbed her fuzzy back. She cooed, making almost a purring noise, and nudged her nose into my hand. From that moment on, I felt an emotional affection for this little dog.

Not being able to feed correctly, the runt had received only minuscule bits of nourishment since she had been born five days earlier. She didn't suck correctly because her tongue turned upward toward the roof of her mouth.

Jill and I tried using a baby bottle to feed the runt but her jaws weren't strong enough to squeeze the tough rubber nipple. Still she showed enough spunk to persuade us to help her fight to live.

"Let's try a doll's bottle, "Jill declared. "We can get one at the bazaar."

Her driver chauffeured us to the historic Grand Bazaar, a huge cavernous building that stretched for several city blocks in all directions. The arched ceilings covered small stalls on both sides of a narrow walkway. Hundreds of vendors shouted at shoppers, hawking their wares and arguing with each other.

Many women wore the black chador. A few women even balanced shiny vessels on their heads as they strolled through the crowded bazaar. Those who had been educated abroad wore Western clothes. Jill and I easily fit in.

Each stall contained something of interest for the strolling shopper: brass, silver, gold, jewelry, baskets, pottery, furniture, toys, clothes, kitchen utensils, carpets, food, and flowers. It was like a Middle Eastern Wal-Mart. In contrast, however, the bazaar never seemed clean. All the items gathered dust as they remained day after day in the hollow halls of the vast building, waiting for customers.

Because Jill walked with me, I felt comfortable and safe. We wore dresses with stylish jackets, and it was obvious to all that we were not Persian.

The Muslim men stared at us. Some even made snide comments. When Jill heard derogatory words, she turned and yelled at them in Farsi. Surprised that she understood their language, they quickly retreated and pretended they had no idea who had said what.

From a nearby mosque we heard loud speakers broadcasting the *azan*, the call to prayer. The sound emanated from one of the two tall minarets that topped the front of each mosque.

Five times a day, about every four hours, Muslims responded to the message and kneeled to face Mecca. They first washed their hands and feet before bowing to pray. This sound intruded upon the lives of all Muslims, no matter who they were with or what they were doing, day or night. A sad wailing prayer called the faithful to fulfill their sacred duties, and then it stopped and the people returned to their day's activities or went back to bed.

During daylight hours, the men walked to the mosque for prayer. Most women stayed at home to pray. At night the faithful would pray in separate areas of their houses. I was surprised to learn that the time for prayer changed every day. Not by much, only by a minute or two, according to the sun's rotation and the exact physical place of the worshiper.

Most of the vendors in the Grand Bazaar were men, thin and clean shaven except for bushy sideburns and mustaches, popular at the time and typical of men throughout the world in the seventies. They held cigarettes, flicking ashes and butts, and continuously smoked while we shopped.

Customers were of both sexes. Some fanatical families, extremely religious in their views, did not allow their women to leave the house. Consequently, the husbands or male servants did the daily shopping.

As we moved through the bazaar, I sometimes heard loud arguing between the vendors and the shoppers. It sounded like heated fights, filled with angry words, their arms and hands flailing in all directions. Throughout the exchange, the words would be punctuated by *Enshalla*, or "God willing."

Jill explained, "This is typical of how locals do business. Don't take it seriously. It's just the Persian way of negotiating."

Toward the back of the bazaar in the children's section, we found a doll's bottle among the games and toys. Even with only one item to purchase, Jill bargained for a lower price. It was the thing to do when shopping and the vendor expected it.

Once the price had been established, the merchant placed the doll's bottle in Jill's shopping bag and nodded to us with the word, "Machakher," or thank you. Paying attention to their verbal exchange, I began to learn Farsi.

Jill's driver, who had been waiting at the curb, drove us back to the house. As we approached the compound, he honked the horn, and a man dressed in loose pants and a flowing top opened the gate. He looked as though he had been taking a nap and that he appeared unhappy at being awakened. The servants worked long hours and often slept when the owners traveled outside the compound — either for shopping or for out-of-town trips.

In the kitchen I listened to the kettle boil and watched the puppies in their enclosure. Jill mixed milk and baby formula for the runt's consumption. The warm smell of the room added to the comfy feeling of our new friendship.

I picked up the tiny puppy and cradled her in the palm of my hand, holding her steady between my fingers. Jill placed the nipple of the doll's bottle above the tongue and between the puppy's parting lips. Although the nipple was in the correct position, the puppy had no energy to suck the formula.

"Let's cut the tip off and try again," I suggested.

This time the runt shifted and began to consume the formula. While I held her, her little paws pushed back and forth as if she were kneading bread. Back and forth. Back and forth. How relieved and excited I felt as I watched her ribcage rise and fall with every breath.

"Wow. Look at that. Boy, was she ever hungry!" I exclaimed.

In my enthusiasm, I let her drink too much. Her little belly extended sideways — almost as wide as my palm. Thank goodness, she burped and spit out some liquid, and I stopped the feeding. From then on, I gave her a bottle of formula every two hours, getting up throughout the night and interrupting my daily home activities.

There was such an emotional pull for me to save this little puppy that I abandoned all common sense. I was determined to rescue her. And thus began the saga of my black Labrador retriever.

I named her Shah Bahnoo Siya. In Farsi the words mean Black Empress. We called her Bahnoo, or Lady, for short.

# Chapter Six
# Varang-E-Rud

"Jill and I are going fishing tomorrow. Probably into the nearby mountains. Want to come?" David asked a few days later.

With the promise of good fishing and unusual photography, we readily agreed.

"Sure," Ron said over his shoulder as he sauntered toward our suite. "We'll get our gear ready."

Sunlight filtered through the beige curtains in our bedroom the next morning. We woke early for the outing to Karaj Dam, forty miles northwest of Tehran. The dam not only supplied water to the city residents and businesses but also to the nearby farms.

Dr. Fred gathered us in his Land Rover for the long ride to the Varang-E-Rud and Dam. Jill, wedged in the middle of the back seat, had David and me on each side of her. Ron sat up front with Fred who pointed out the numerous historic and ecological highlights along the way.

Jill and I bonded over the quest to save the little puppy. We talked nonstop about what we'd do next to help Bahnoo's struggle to live. Our chat on the drive was typical.

"Do you think Bahnoo will make it?" I asked her as we drove north through the dismal early morning light.

"I don't know. She's sure trying."

"Yup. I can tell. She's definitely a fighter."

Before long the divided highway narrowed to a two-lane dirt road that spiraled upward, snaking its way into the mountains. Fred drove through expansive dry lands dotted with scrub brush, up narrow winding roads, and past tiny villages covered in dust.

In the distance, we saw mini sandstorms rolling across the horizon. Along the way to the foothills of the snow-covered Alborz Mountains, we stopped to talk with several managers of

Iran's Department of the Protection to the Environment, similar to the Fish and Wildlife Service in the United States.

We greeted each other with *salom*, or hello, as we entered the agency offices. I noticed most of the employees drank tea or coffee and smoked nonstop. Their tanned and heavily lined, dark faces had been grizzled by sun and cigarettes. As soon as they brushed ashes off their trousers, they relit another cigarette. Thick smoke filled their small, dingy offices. I coughed and hacked and often excused myself for some fresh air outside.

As customary, the managers offered us tea and Turkish coffee whenever we stopped. Because it's offensive not to accept their offer, we paused for a chat and had a few cups. I requested coffee which they served in chunky, two-inch high, cream-colored ceramic cups that were placed on miniature saucers. The dense, almost solid liquid looked like black mud. I added a spoonful of sugar to dilute the mixture and brought the hot drink to my lips.

Most of the men drank tea. It was served in a small clear glass enclosed in a decorative metal container, known as an *estacon*. They drank it as hot as one could stand and finished it quickly. The men swallowed the almost-boiling tea while holding a white sugar cube either between their teeth or inside their cheeks. The compressed cube dissolved slowly and they added more sugar as they sipped; their tea turned overly sweet as they consumed the liquid.

I took another sip of hot coffee, trying not to burn my tongue, and watched the men manipulate the cube of sugar while swallowing their tea. From drinking all the liquid during the many office visits on our way to the river, I felt drowned in a sea of sugary black coffee.

"David, could you ask if I can use a restroom?" I said.

He spoke in Farsi to the group of men. Shortly thereafter, a young female arrived wearing a black chador and directed me to the bathroom.

As I approached the room, I stopped, repelled by the stench. But I had to go. There in the small, cement floor was a six-inch-diameter hole, surrounded by streams of urine. Gagging, I entered and attempted to pee. Between the overwhelming smells and biting flies, I couldn't continue. I left the room and hoped for another chance to go before I had an embarrassing accident.

Once we reached the Varang-E-Rud, I walked behind some bushes and did my business.

Having camped for many years in the California Sierras, I believed going in the woods was much more hygienic than using a local's bathroom.

Before we began fishing, we enjoyed a picnic of sandwiches and cookies put together by the Laylins' houseboy. He had enclosed the goodies in a wicker basket and added a thick rug for us to sit on. The day soon warmed as the sun rose. Jill and Fred sat on rocks, off to the side smoking their cigarettes.

After a short pause, the five of us donned our waders, clinched our belts, and crossed a shallow section of the river. Once we adjusted our fishing gear, we climbed a heavily-used trail through a mountain crevice to reach another section of the stream.

Local men with loaded donkeys passed us along the way as they trekked further into the mountains toward their villages. Very few trees and stark, grey-brown landscape surrounded us on this lengthy, high desert journey.

Before long, large cumulus clouds jostled against each other and rolled across the darkening sky. A slow rain fell in a steady thin curtain. The damp smell surrounded us as we dropped down into the valley to reach a better spot to fish.

With the river high and murky, fishing was poor, and I had nothing to photograph. The rain stopped, and we crossed the river again to return to the truck.

"Why don't we drive toward the mouth of the reservoir," David suggested to Fred. "We'll find clear water there."

As the Rover moved over the soggy dirt road, Fred shifted into low gear. In time, however, the wheels became stuck and refused to turn. The muddy path had become too deep and too thick.

We abandoned the vehicle and got out to push. Fred manipulated the gears and steered as the four of us shoved. In a few minutes we freed the truck but fly fishing in such a dirty river became almost impossible.

David, Fred, and Ron hiked to the reservoir's dam while Jill and I stayed and fished where we were. We were determined to prove the men wrong. Eventually we took a break and sat on rocks at the edge of the river. The fish had not cooperated, and we had nothing to show for our time. Jill dug into her pocket and pulled out a cigarette. She lit it and leaned back, blowing smoke into the air.

"I'm originally from Connecticut, but now live in California," I told Jill. "Where are you from?"

"My family's from England, but I was born in Zambia," she responded. "Do you know Zambia?"

"Yes. We just returned from Africa a few months back. I was also there five years ago when I visited Kenya and South Africa."

"What were you doing then?"

"I used to be a stewardess and took a four-month leave of absence, hitchhiking around the world," I answered. "It was a great time to travel. It still is."

"I've done a lot of traveling myself," Jill commented. "Mostly in Europe and the southern part of Africa. David and I met in Monaco — at one of those plush casinos. You know, the ones that require full-length formals and the men wear tuxes."

Before long Jill stubbed her cigarette on a rock and flicked the butt into the fast moving river. The air had turned cold. We wanted to warm ourselves inside the Rover and followed the direction the men had taken to retrieve the truck keys.

As I walked along the side of the river, the mud became deeper and less dense. It seemed to have swallowed my legs like a whirlpool of sludge. I sank to my calves, embedded, and couldn't budge.

"Jill. Help! I can't move," I yelled.

In the initial twilight, Jill inched along on her hands and knees, the belly of her waders rubbing over the spongy dirt. She reached out and grasped my outstretched hand. I struggled forward as she pulled with all her might.

Suddenly, we heard a loud slurping sound. The thick muck had released me. Cold and wet, we crawled across the smelly sludge, struggling to reach firmer ground.

When Jill and I caught up with David and Ron, we were breathless and coated from head to toe with mud. Even in the poor light, they knew we were not happy. Fred was no longer there; he had left the men an hour earlier. He had decided to return his fishing gear and to move the truck for easier access.

The evening dusk had now begun to settle throughout the valley. Loose gravel and rock chips crunched beneath our feet as we left the river and started up the mountain. We picked our way through the brush and rocks and trekked upward.

"Watch out for snakes," cautioned David. "Poisonous ones are everywhere."

"Great," I thought. "I can barely see in front of me, and now I have to avoid snakes! Thank goodness for thick waders."

Before long, darkness had snagged us on the steep cliff. The four of us struggled up the mountainside, but we had become lost in the last of the day's light. Slowly we climbed and eventually found a decent path. We hiked in total blackness along the ridge, back toward the car.

We saw the lights from the Rover slicing through the tree tops on the other side of the river and moved in that direction. Finally, we descended to the swift river after sliding between rock crevices along the side of the mountain. Fred shined truck lights on the river and called to us, encouraging us to follow his directions.

"Here! Here's the spot to cross," he shouted above the noise of the rushing water.

In the dark, the four of us clinched our wader belts tight and wrapped our arms together. Ron and David flanked Jill and me as we stepped into the dark torrent. We began to cross the swiftly moving river, holding our fishing rods high and taking one baby step after another, facing down river, our backs to the current.

"Hang on tight," Ron yelled to me over the crash of the waves as he grabbed my arm.

I felt the icy grip of fear seize me. Drops of perspiration rippled down my spine as I held on to Jill and Ron with all my might. Terrified of falling into the river, we shuffled our way to the opposite side.

Once we reached the shore, we washed our waders at the river's edge, cleaned our gear, and climbed into the truck. Fred, thinking he had been helping, had moved the Rover closer to us. However, it was on the other side of the river. Crossing the rough Varang-E-Rud in complete darkness was a passage none of us ever wanted to repeat.

From sheer exhaustion, we collapsed onto our truck seats and began the long ride down the gravel road toward Tehran. Clouds of dust unfurled from the few vehicles ahead of us. I noticed that even at night, no other cars had their lights on. As we approached an intersection, cars would flash their bright lights, blinding the oncoming drivers.

Stirring from my stupor in the backseat, I asked Fred, "Why are they driving without lights?"

Before answering, he continued to maneuver the Land Rover around tight twisting curves of this narrow road with no side railings. Steep drops greeted any vehicle that went over the edge.

"The dust from the road makes it difficult to see. It's like driving in fog. They turn their lights off so they can see better," he replied.

"And they flash their lights at crossroads," David added, "because they want the oncoming drivers to realize another car is approaching the intersection. They don't realize the havoc they create with their bright lights."

The driver's perilous procedures caused several vehicles to be damaged and stranded on this dangerous mountain road. Some of the cars and trucks have been left there for months and looked like they had been frozen in time.

Finally we arrived in Tehran. I checked on the puppies and saw that Bahnoo had been well cared for during my absence. After showering and changing into casual clothes, the four of us enjoyed an evening by the fire. David served drinks and Ali Akbar brought in popcorn. Before long Sable and Boots, the male Lab, joined in our nightly ritual, all of us warm and cozy in front of a blazing fire.

# Chapter Seven
# The Compound

"The compound must be checked daily," David advised me several days later. "Tribal people periodically throw poison over our walls. They believe dogs are unclean — impure actually."

"You mean they want to kill your dogs... even though they don't do any harm?" I asked. "They don't even bark."

"The Koran warns Muslims against any contact with dogs," he answered. "Some Muslims even have their so-called pets euthanized during religious holidays. Or they kill the animals outright. It's disgusting!"

Hearing these religious principles from David made it all the more meaningful that his Muslim servants looked after the dogs. They fed them and scrubbed their kennels. Even the woman who sewed the clothes, cleaned the house, and washed the laundry took a special interest in the puppies, especially Bahnoo. She hand fed her whenever Jill and I couldn't be at home.

No commercial dog food was available in Iran during the seventies. Consequently, once the puppies were weaned, Ali Akbar was responsible for the dogs' dinners. He chopped up meat and blended it with eggs, oil, rice, and bread. All the puppies and adult dogs looked like show animals because of Ali Akbar's special skills. Their coats were shiny, they seemed happy, and they had an abundance of energy.

A week or so later, on one particular night during our evening ritual, a fire glowed in the living room fireplace. David prepared drinks, and Ali Akbar brought in the Labradors and popcorn. The squirming puppies soon learned that the little round balls of popcorn were fun to catch and good to chew. They scooted around each other, trying to be the first to grasp the tiny butter balls. Surprisingly, Bahnoo would pick up a piece of popcorn and bring it to me. She was already retrieving and not even four weeks old.

Ron and I sat on the floor to play with the dogs, and I watched Bahnoo wiggle over to me, her whole body twisting in the process. Although Jill and I had taken turns feeding her, she bonded with me and I with her. Labradors, when a strong attachment is developed, are intensely loyal. They form a tremendous trust and seem to crave constant companionship.

Bahnoo leaped on my legs, trying to scramble up my body. I reached down and brought her to my chest, cradling her in my arms and turning her over to rub her belly. I heard a familiar purring noise as she looked at me with her soulful eyes. I put my face to her body, smelling the scent that only puppies have — one of warm milk and baby fur.

Since David had released his secretary a few weeks earlier, I had taken her place. Every work day I sat at a desk in the Iran Safaris office, typing letters and filing correspondence. Because the Iranian women who worked in the office were fluent in English, we had no problems communicating. They were eager to learn progressive ways of office production and business etiquette. They also wanted to know more about the customs, clothes, and culture of the United States.

In turn, I learned Farsi numbers and various words and phrases, both in speaking and in writing. If one of the secretaries slipped back into a native expression, I heard the slight click of her tongue as she raised her head. This sound and gesture meant, "No." She would be denying someone's request.

After lunch Jill and I often shopped. She had spent weeks looking for lamps to decorate her home. The local stores offered limited selections, and each lamp cost over a hundred dollars (or in today's prices, over a thousand dollars).

As we strolled along the sidewalk, a transit bus rumbled down the street, smoke billowing from its exhaust pipes. The air turned thick and smelled of diesel fumes. Jill and I were immediately enveloped in a gray cloud and covered our mouths and noses to prevent breathing in the toxic emissions.

We watched chador-covered women walking ahead of us, their black coverings flapping in the breeze. They reminded me of strutting crows, parading down a footpath. The sidewalk soon became clogged with shoppers and squatting vendors. Before long, we heard the sound of bicycle bells. Jill and I turned, moving to the side as the rider rushed by. The clopping from donkey's feet kept us near the building walls as a merchant and his supplies passed us on the walkway.

Except for a few women from the countryside, the faces of the Tehran women were mostly visible. The rural women, however, added a scarf around their heads that completely shielded their faces except for a small horizontal slit. Only their eyes, not even their eyebrows, were allowed to be shown.

Surprisingly, the secretaries discarded their dark coverings the moment they arrived at the Iran Safaris office. When they removed their enormous chadors, they showed plunging necklines and skimpy miniskirts.

"Who would have thought?" I whispered to Jill. "They seem so demure, hidden under their chadors."

On an alternate road, I saw several large Persian carpets stretched across the street. Cars drove over them, supposedly to age them for the Western market. Silk rugs were never placed on the road; they were too delicate to take the vehicle beating.

"That reminds me," I said. "Let's look at some carpets. I want to buy a Persian carpet before we leave Iran."

We entered a nearby shop that specialized in tribal products. A salesman showed us carpet samplings that had been woven by the Bakhtiari tribe. Persian rugs are classified by the place they are woven. The nomadic Bakhtiari were from the Southwestern part of Iran. From the pictures the salesman showed us, I saw that the men wore black sheered, lamb's wool caps on their heads. The people were quite handsome with almost a European look. He told me the Persian people are known as Caucasian, not Arabic.

The salesman informed us that the cheapest carpets were made of pure wool. A medium-priced carpet was made of a wool and silk blend. And the most expensive ones were made entirely of silk. These luxurious rugs would only be used as wall hangings.

"Silk is way too fragile to be placed on a floor," he said. "It's very expensive. However, the thicker the material, the price becomes more economical and is made faster.

"For example," he added, "An average nine- by twelve-foot, wool carpet with three hundred knots per square inch takes a year to complete. That means the carpet I'm showing you would take a year for six weavers to finish it."

Now I had a dilemma. I wanted a Persian rug, but Ron and I didn't have enough money in our budget to buy a wool and silk blend. If I had not learned about the differences in the weaves and knots, I would have been happy buying a less expensive carpet. I decided to procrastinate. I would not buy anything that day.

# Chapter Eight
# Bandar Pahlavi Safari Lodge

Ron's travel alarm went off at 6:30 a.m. I opened my eyes to look at the clock and then buried my head under the pillows. It was November 8 and Ron began singing "Happy Birthday." His voice was soft and pleasant as he sang the traditional song. Pleased that he remembered, I slowly raised my head and kissed him. We would be enjoying another great day in Iran with Jill and David, this time at the Bandar Pahlavi Safari Lodge.

He looked at his watch and noticed we were late for breakfast. I jumped into the shower and toweled off before binding my long hair into a ponytail. Since we were going to the mountains, I dressed in a turtleneck sweater with jeans, and pulled on leather boots. Then I checked on Bahnoo.

She was snuggled under Sable's front leg, nestled among her seven chubby siblings.

"Just a moment, Ron. I need to give Bahnoo her morning bottle," I said.

As I cradled her in the crook of my left arm, I grasped the bottle Ali Akbar had prepared. She was as hungry as usual, even though she was now taking Sable's nipple. Her morning and evening bottles were still offered since she needed to gain more weight.

Once my chores were finished, David drove the four of us to Bandar Pahlavi, a port in Northern Iran. We were going to celebrate my birthday in style. Iran Safaris owned a topnotch lodge located on the Caspian Sea, the world's largest saltwater lake.

The road had a light layer of pavement as we traveled north through an area of flat, hard-packed dirt. The blank palette of the desert, stretching out on either side of the roadway, added to the starkness. We saw nothing but a lone mesquite tree along this particular dry area of Iran.

In the distance a few villages dotted the landscape, and local men came out to the road to sell their town's wares. Pottery in many shapes and sizes, from small cups to three-foot-high vases, gathered dust on the side of the road. Most were plain with a brownish gray hue but a few had elaborate flower and bird designs. Another vendor had baskets, hats, brooms, and mats hanging from posts stuck in the ground.

"The village men and women handmade these from native grasses," David informed us as he pointed to the baskets. "They get the grass from the marshes around the Caspian Sea."

In another hour we had crossed the scrub-dotted desert, and dust had consumed our vehicle. We had opted to keep the windows open so as not to suffocate from the stifling hot air, but the wispy sand had covered us — our hair, clothes, and luggage.

Once we left the desert behind, we passed small herds of sheep and goats attended by young boys, often riding on donkeys guiding their flocks to better feeding grounds. The rising highway turned and twisted, and the mountainside became greener.

We drove through a dozen arched tunnels, their channel passages built of russet-colored stone and mud. A few people walked the road with colorful shawls wrapped around their faces, the ends of the material flapping in the dirty breeze. Donkeys stirred alongside the moving travelers, carrying supplies to local villages.

In another hour we drove up the winding, steep foothills of the Elborz Mountains, my eyes glued to the road ahead. Many, many cars and trucks had been abandoned along the way. The vehicles had moved too close to the road's edge, their front wheels balancing outward toward the deep abyss. At every turn I prayed another vehicle would not cross to our side of the road, pushing us off the narrow roadway.

"Are you OK?" Ron asked as he glanced back at my white face.

"I'm fine. I'm just a little queasy from all the turns and twists, but I'll be OK," I answered as I tilted my head out the window to catch a breath of fresh air. Soon a subtle cooling breeze blew in from the north, and we began our descent toward the Iran Safaris lodge, located at sea level.

Before long we turned off the main highway and stopped at a gate at the end of a gravel road. A lodge guard emerged to wave us through. The area was surrounded by cypress and a few deciduous trees. We had now entered the Caspian Sea flats, an area surrounding the saltwater lake.

Once the four of us arrived at the picturesque hunting lodge, we piled out, and uniformed assistants carried our luggage to nearby cabins. We quickly unpacked and put on fishing waders. I added a ski parka to give warmth to my body already chilled by the cool mountain air.

Following a couple hours of pike fishing, we returned to the lodge. After changing once again for dinner, we entered the main building. The large reception area looked just like a hunting lodge should: Persian carpets, mounted animal heads, rifles displayed on wood brackets, cocktails, and caviar. The side tables were layered with half-empty vodka glasses, cigarette-filled ashtrays, and decorative hors d'oeuvres.

Our dinner that night was excellent. We enjoyed a delicious four-course dinner of salad, creamed tomato soup, sturgeon soufflé, and birthday cake. French wines complimented each course. The lodge chef had only remote vegetable and dairy produce available for his cooking preparations, yet he had created an outstanding meal that would rival most four-star restaurants.

After breakfast the next day, we again went fishing, this time for gigantic catfish. With no luck David changed our itinerary, and we spent the afternoon flushing out snipe from nearby rice paddies. Ron killed four birds and offered them to his guide to take home for dinner.

Afterwards we tried pigeon hunting, and then we hunted for pheasants in pale fields nearby. Now that was exciting. The birds flushed right at my feet, scaring me in the process. I never did coordinate the release of the trigger's safety catch in enough time to actually get off a shot. The birds burst into the air, lucky to have me as their only nearby hunter.

Very early the following morning we faced a cold, moisture-rich sky swirling above us. The stiff breeze hinted of snow. Ron and David left before the sun was up to duck hunt along the Caspian Sea. As they scrambled into the Land Rover, I could see their smoky breaths streaming into the air. I stood in the doorway of the cottage, watching them and shivering.

Their guides had dressed warmly in padded khaki uniforms and placed shotguns into the storage area of the Rover. Chilled from a blast of icy mountain air, I retreated to my bed as soon as they had left.

The men who flushed the birds, beaters as they were called, wore old, weathered jackets that had long since lost their color. When the group returned from a snow-filled morning, I discovered that Ron and David had had fabulous hunting. They returned with many ducks of several breeds, and David asked the lodge's cook to prepare them for the dinner that night.

"There are two Italian princes staying at the lodge this week," David mentioned while we enjoyed cocktails later that day.

"They probably bought their titles," Jill added. "Many Italians do that and then come here expecting to be treated like royalty."

"We treat everyone the same – whether they are royalty or not," David said as he sipped his vodka.

As the evening wore on, white-shirted waiters circulated in the crowded reception area with a tray of toast, lemon, and black beads of caviar. The soft, pea-sized eggs were from the Beluga sturgeon, a fish that had been swimming a few hours earlier in the Caspian Sea. The eggs arrived in glass dishes and then were served with mother-of-pearl teaspoons.

"Metal spoons would have influenced the taste and are never used," Jill said as she showed me how to perform the fish egg tasting routine.

"Drop the caviar on a piece of toast. Then squeeze on a little lemon," she added. "Now, take a sip of vodka. It'll cleanse your pallet."

The toast had its crust removed and was cut into small triangle wedges. Lemon slices lined a nearby ceramic plate, and the frosted Russian vodka had been thickened to an icy syrup. Once the routine had been established, one repeated the process, again and again.

While a fire blazed in the large hearth, a dozen hunters surrounded David and listened to his tales of hunting and fishing in the nearby mountains. Dressed in camouflage clothes, he stood in the center of the guests with his vodka glass at his lips and held court.

The men were mesmerized by his stories. He mentioned gazelle, mountain sheep, and bear, as well as assorted birds and fish. Sitting on a nearby couch, I bent forward, craning to hear his every word.

All of a sudden the lodge door exploded open, breaking into my thoughts. A red-faced man stormed into the room.

"You said there would be ducks! Where were they?" he screamed in a white-hot rage.

He jumped on David's back, furious that the heavy snow had disrupted his hunt. He wrapped his shotgun around David's neck and pulled back with his hands, gagging and choking David in the process.

The waiters wrestled the enraged hunter to the floor and helped David regain his stance. Drinks and hors d'oeuvres scattered as the guests scrambled to avoid the chaos.

Ron, Jill, and I stood like zombies, watching the drama from the other side of the room, astonished by such conflict. For a few seconds, the weight of silence filled the air. David bent over and brushed off his clothes, embarrassed by the disruptive episode.

"This has never happened before," David said, coughing to clear his throat.

The dark-haired man began yelling again and rushed David from the other side of the room. This time he hugged him and apologized for his inappropriate action. The two friends stood in the center of the room, wrapped in each other arms, laughing at the crazy encounter.

The guests chatted with each other about the rowdy incident and soon retired to the dining room. Although the initial chatter within the room had subdued, our excellent dinner of fresh ducks in an orange and wine sauce quickly made up for the hunter's raucous and unusual behavior.

# Chapter Nine
# Delhi, India

David pulled a map of Nepal from a tall file cabinet and spread it across his desk. He showed Ron and me the route from Kathmandu to the fertile Himalayan foothills.

Tiger Tops Lodge sat in the Chitwan National Park, surrounded by dense jungles below the tallest mountains in the world. We leaned forward, bent over the map, and listened to his stories of elephant trekking, tiger spotting, and fly fishing.

"I'll bottle feed Bahnoo for the next two weeks," Jill said as she entered the office.

"Thanks, Jill. She won't need much," I replied.

Now over a month old, Bahnoo required only a little additional food as Sable regularly nursed her. Still the runt of the litter, she had developed into an active puppy and eagerly fought for her place at Sable's ample belly.

At 10 the following morning, Ron and I boarded a plane for Nepal, another planned stop on our round-the-world trip. Nepal required visas for us to enter their country. Because San Francisco did not have a consulate, and Tehran could not arrange visas within our time frame, Ron and I deplaned in New Delhi, India, to obtain one. We also needed to renew our Iranian visas now that we were staying beyond the tourist permit period.

We landed just as the noon sun appeared in the sky above the capital city. From the moment we left the terminal, India saturated our senses. Ron stared with wonder at the unusual sights, sounds, and scents of his first encounter in this remarkable country.

The porter and I followed Ron's long strides to a waiting taxi. On our drive to the hotel, we noticed an array of colors. Vendors draped metal rods above sari shops with red, turquoise, orange, and yellow materials. Even the passing buildings, bicycles, and cabs were painted with a variety of rainbow hues. Brilliant colors were intense and everywhere.

When Ron and I strolled outside the hotel that evening, we saw sleeping bodies curled under blankets beside the brick wall, a barrier that separated the hotel grounds from the public. Men huddled around metal cans filled with fire, their faces bathed in the light of the reflected flames.

Several cripples sat on the sidewalk and stretched out their hands, pleading for money. After donating a few coins, more beggars came toward us, and we became uncomfortable and retreated to the security of our hotel.

We woke at eight the next day to miserable smog. The air hung heavy with diesel fumes, and the haze was so thick, it reminded me of San Francisco fog. We could barely see across the narrow park in front of the hotel. There were too many ancient automobiles within this congested city to absorb its massive vehicle pollution.

After breakfast we took a three-wheel, open mini-cab to the Iran Embassy to renew our visa. I felt like we were on Coney Island, taking an amusement ride as our cab dodged between people, vehicles, and sacred cows. The cabby of this tiny taxi honked constantly as if keeping beat while he maneuvered through the shifting crowds.

From there we walked to the American Embassy, a beautiful modern structure with green lawns, shade trees, and a sparkling fountain. In the front draped a shining American flag, hanging from the top of a tall white pole. It felt good to see our Stars and Stripes proudly displayed in this very foreign land.

"What are the requirements for us to ship a dog from Iran to the United States?" I inquired once we met with an official inside the building. "She'll fly from Tehran to New York City," I added.

"The dog must be between three and six months old. And its papers must be signed by a qualified veterinarian," the male receptionist answered.

He handed me a list of appropriate inoculations, and said, "It must have these vaccinations."

Bahnoo would qualify once she had her shots and the Iranian veterinarian signed her health certificate. I would make an appointment with the Laylins' vet as soon as we returned to Tehran.

Next Ron and I visited the Royal Nepalese Embassy to obtain our required visas. We paid a dollar more, literally under the counter, to receive the paperwork that day. The uniformed official introduced us to an illegal money changer down the hall from his office. We traded American dollars for Nepalese rupees, a black market transaction that took place right inside the embassy building.

From there, Ron and I took a three-wheeled bicycle cab, peddled by a middle-aged man, into Old Delhi. Bright blue fringe edged the red top that shaded the two seats, and florescent pink and green tape covered the bicycle frame. We passed vividly painted shops and women in stunning saris. Once again we were blasted by brilliant colors.

There are hundreds of different languages spoken within India. As a result, the government mandated English and Hindi as the official languages. Consequently, we had no trouble communicating while we toured and collected our visas.

Dusk settled in the old walled city once we arrived in this teeming shopping area. It looked like an uncovered superstore. Everything one ever wanted was crammed into both sides of the restricted roadway. Packed throughout the narrow streets were vast numbers of bicycles, people, cows, and mini-cabs.

Ron required additional grease for his fishing reels and searched the area for a mechanical vendor. When he requested grease from the merchant, he made a prayer-like gesture with his hands by forming his fingers into a steeple, the universal signal of goodwill. Dressed in a beige shirt and a white turban, the man held up his palms and refused to let Ron pay.

"Please. All I want is a thank you," the Sikh said as he swished his head from side to side, the Indian way of indicating approval or appreciation.

"What a nice surprise," I thought. It was another gesture of kindness that we continually received from the locals.

As Ron and I walked toward the main road and left the crowded shopping area, two small boys wearing rags with no shoes approached me. They touched my arm and looked up at me. When I responded, they giggled and ran away. I handed several coins to a few crippled children and to some amputees on two-foot boards fitted with rollers. They looked like teenagers, except they were skateboarding without legs.

Once I opened my purse, a dozen older beggars ambushed us. We quickly became uncomfortable in the newly-formed crowd. They surrounded us, their hands extended, pleading as they called to us, "Please. Please."

Begging also with their eyes and pulling at our clothes, they sucked us into their mob. I held my purse to my chest and turned away. We stepped from the swarm, and the circling children and amputees quickly evaporated. Our jostling beggars soon attached themselves to fresh Westerners walking into Old Delhi.

# Chapter Ten
# India Five Years Earlier

The next morning Ron and I took a local bus to Agra, the site of the Taj Mahal. The hotel had given us directions to a bus stop near its entrance. The elaborate memorial was a setting I knew Ron would want to visit, and I was ready to see it again.

Five years earlier in 1967, I had made a trip to the Taj Mahal, joining several Europeans on a bus tour arranged by the InterContinental Hotel. Outside the barrier walls of this famous monument, lay sick, disfigured, and maimed people, all of them wearing rags and begging for money. Many had stumped limbs or leprosy. These people were known as the *untouchables*. Some, without feet or legs, sat on boards fitted with rollers so they could move from spot to spot, a poor man's wheelchair. We had been told that many untouchable children were disfigured at birth, thereby creating better beggars for their families.

The caste system stated four levels to the Hindu social order: preachers and teachers were at the top; government workers and soldiers were next; merchants, artists, and farmers followed; and laborers were at the bottom. The level not mentioned because it was too low to be considered was the untouchables, the men who cleaned the sewers, emptied the garbage, and removed dead animals. That is, if they could obtain a job at all.

After the tour and early the following day, I was supposed to travel to Pakistan on a space-available pass. I arrived at the New Delhi airport at five in the morning, boarded the flight, and relaxed in my seat.

"Miss Phelps. Please ring your call button."

The announcement came over the PA system, and I did as I was requested. When the flight attendant reached me, she said, "You have to deplane now. We have a paying customer."

As an airline employee, I paid only 10 percent of the commercial ticket price. However, flying "space available" meant I could be removed from the plane if a full-paying customer arrived. The crew had my suitcase at the front of the aircraft along with a receipt for the next flight, which would not depart for a couple of days. Now, what was I to do?

Back at the hotel I waited in the lobby for the previous day's tour driver to open his office. He was the only person I knew in India, and I barely knew him. Once he unlocked his front door, I walked into his office and explained my forced departure from the airplane. He turned to face me as he walked toward his desk.

"What can I do to help?" he asked.

"Do you know of a youth hostel or a less expensive hotel for me?" I asked. "It'll only be for a couple of days."

A slim man with smooth black hair, dark eyes, and a friendly smile, reintroduced himself.

"My name is Yaj. I remember you from yesterday."

We shook hands, and he gestured to the chair in front of his desk. I slipped into the seat, and he picked up the phone and dialed a number. He spoke quickly into the mouthpiece, faced sideways, and then turned toward me with a large smile across his face.

"You'll stay with us. My wife and I would be honored."

"Really? Are you sure? I don't want to be a bother. Thank you so much," I blurted all at once.

"You'll be by yourself for the next few hours until I can leave work. Chandra is very happy to meet you," he said as he moved his head from side to side, beaming the whole time.

Later that day we boarded Yaj's scooter, piled my suitcase on the back rack, and took off for his home in the outskirts of New Delhi. The narrow streets of the jammed city were clogged with vehicles.

We threaded our way through handcarts and wagons and roared past cars and trucks, weaving in and out of traffic as vehicles belched noxious exhaust fumes. I held on to the chrome safety sidebars for dear life. The noise from blaring horns and screeching brakes assaulted my ears, but there was no way I'd let go of the sidebars to shield my ears.

"What have I gotten into?" I thought as I suffered through the madness.

Yaj's second floor apartment had three rooms: a living room, bedroom, and bathroom (with both a Western toilet and a hole in the tiled floor below a spout near the floor). The kitchen on the roof was shared by several families.

The fear of fire kept almost all Indian kitchens in either separate structures or on rooftops. The cooking area looked out over the desert; its tar-covered roof crisscrossed with sagging lines, overloaded with colorful clothes drying in the breeze.

The twelve-foot-square living room was furnished with a loveseat, two side tables plus lamps, and a couple of red-cushioned wooden chairs. A small refrigerator filled a spot in the corner and indicated to their guests that Yaj's family was wealthy enough to own a modern appliance.

Chandra, a beautiful woman with light olive skin, wore a bright yellow and orange sari and had her thick black hair oiled and braided into a single plait hanging down her back. A colorful silk shawl covered her head and most of her hair.

From the time I arrived, it was like Grand Central Station. The tinkle of tiny bells on open-toed shoes and the jingling of bangle bracelets announced that neighbors and friends had arrived at the opened apartment door to meet the American woman staying at Yaj's house.

They came in droves and crowded into the living room. Everyone greeted me with palms together, fingers pointed upward in a prayerful gesture. They bowed slightly from the waist. I stood, duplicating the greeting, and then returned to one of the chairs.

They spoke English and asked continuous questions, laughing at my answers. Both Chandra and Yaj were college graduates as were most of the contemporaries who came to visit. They were considered the new middle class of India.

That night Yaj slept on the couch in the living room, and Chandra and I shared a double bed in the adjacent room. The bed consisted of ropes tied in a square pattern with a sheet over the ropes, another sheet to cover ourselves, and two pillows. The night temperature hovered close to 80 degrees; consequently, we never used a blanket.

While we lay next to each other in the double bed, Chandra asked never-ending questions about my personal life and about the customs, music, and clothes of the American people.

"Why are you traveling by yourself?"

She was a married woman who never went shopping without her husband. In comparison, I was a single working woman, a flight attendant, traveling around the world by myself.

"Why was I not married?"

"What was it like to work in the airline industry, flying from country to country?"

We talked until two in the morning like teenagers at a sleepover. Every time I turned around, my elbow protruded through the four-inch squares formed by the ropes. In Colonial times most Americans had rope beds. The expression "sleep tight" came from the use of these beds. The tighter the ropes, the firmer the foundation, and the easier it was to sleep.

Early the next morning Yaj needed to ask Chandra a question. She rose from the bed, completely clad in her two-piece pajama set, and quickly covered her head. I was surprised at her immediate modesty when it was only her husband at the bedroom door.

"Because you are present," Chandra told me, "I covered my head to show respect to Yaj."

"When my work ends, we can show Bobbi the sights of New Delhi," Yaj suggested while he was at the bedroom door. "Tell her my uncle is the National Museum's curator. We'll visit the museum today, but after hours."

That late afternoon the three of us crammed onto Yaj's scooter. Yaj steered with Chandra behind him. I sat behind her, both of us riding with our legs draped over the left side, holding onto the metal rails. This type of commuting was not unusual. We saw many people traveling with three or four people crammed onto one small scooter — some even carrying a baby in a basket up front.

We had a private tour of the museum, and then the uncle treated us to a special dinner at an upscale restaurant. He regarded me as did so many others as a visiting celebrity.

Before long, my time with Chandra and Yaj was over. If it hadn't been for the extra days spent at their home, I would have left India feeling depressed by the overwhelming pollution and poverty. They created a remarkable experience for me. One that made a return visit all the more agreeable.

# Chapter Eleven
# Taj Mahal

Five years later, Ron and I traveled south on a regional bus to see the Taj Mahal. No air conditioning existed, and we stuffed ourselves between other passengers into wood-slated seats.

We bounced along the highway to Agra, the site of the famous monument. The vehicle held men, women, children, piglets, and chickens, as well as baskets of food and supplies. Having rarely seen Westerners on their local bus, the passengers stared at us as if we were from Mars.

On top of the bus, an array of baggage filled every available space. Luggage, livestock crates, tires, furniture, and men jammed the crown of the old vehicle. Everything was tied down, and all the men on top held on to thick ropes.

With no air conditioning the passengers opened the windows. Blowing sand stung our faces while small particles of grit burned our eyes. Once again, I had talked Ron into traveling by local transportation. And once again, he complained of the strange and uncomfortable situation.

After four hours we exited the bus and walked a dirt road toward the monument. Dust swirled around us, and the Agra market became a haze of pale yellow. Looking around me, I saw shawls covering local women waving in the dirty breeze. I turned my head to avoid the blowing sand and noticed a skinny cow lying in the street, its bones revealed below its thin hide. Piles of dung appeared among the rotting food. Locals had thrown garbage into the road for the cows' consumption. Flies and dust saturated the nearby vendors along with the wares they wanted to sell.

Heat visibly rose from the road as Ron and I flowed with a stream of tourists, picking our way across the rubble. Gradually, we left the poverty and dust of the Agra market and walked through the thick, blue-tiled entrance arch of the Taj's surrounding wall.

As soon as Ron and I emerged from under the dark arch, bright sunlight revealed the aqua reflecting pool in front of the Taj. The impressive site swiftly erased the rough images outside the walls.

We held hands and walked on one side of the long, tranquil waterway. In the distance we saw the sparkling white marble monument. The brilliant building inlaid with semi-precious jewels, its huge onion dome towering above us, took my breath away. The striking contrast between the poverty outside and the beauty within was intense.

During the 1600s, the Jahan Emperor ruled almost one-fourth of the world's population. Although he had three wives, he was devoted to Mumtaz Mahai. In their nineteen years together, she had fourteen children. She died during childbirth with the last baby. The Taj Mahal was built in her memory.

After sightseeing and returning to Delhi, Ron and I spent the rest of the day strolling through the old part of the city. We couldn't help but notice how beautiful most Indian women dressed. They wore tight-fitting, colored bodices that were embroidered with sequins and tiny mirrors. As they moved, the sequins and mirrors sparkled in the sunlight. Their arms and ankles were covered with gold and silver bangles, and their long dark hair frequently hung in a single heavy braid. As they aged, some of the women lost their beauty but not their cheerfulness. Whenever we conversed with them, they were always so delightful.

The Sikh men also caught our eyes. Because they never cut their hair, it was wrapped each day in a topknot above their foreheads and then secured inside a twelve-foot-long turban. Their religious edicts created an accepting tolerance of all nationalities and religions. The Sikh men acknowledged women almost as their equals. Their honesty and cheerfulness were easily detected and appreciated.

Dusk soon overcame us, and the small street narrowed to only five feet wide. At the end of the dirt and gravel road, a man held a bear on a string with a brass ring through its nose. The bear's teeth and claws had been removed, and his slobbering mouth looked hideous with nothing but pink gums and flapping jowls. The man and bear danced together while he begged for money. Disgusted by the cruelty, we turned our backs and walked away.

At the main section of Old Delhi, Ron and I encountered a snake charmer among the rows of spice vendors. With his long pipe moving back and forth, he seemed to mesmerize the swaying cobra who mimicked the pipe's movement. We dropped a few rupees into his basket and walked to the curb, catching a cab back to our hotel.

# Chapter Twelve
# Tiger Tops, Nepal

As the next day warmed, Ron and I checked out of the hotel, climbed into a taxi, and headed to the New Delhi airport. Typical of our experiences in Iran and India, the cab driver honked the whole time as he drove through the heavy traffic.

Once the airplane lifted into the air and leveled off, I put my guidebook away and peered out the window. I watched India's flat, dry land disappear as we headed north to the tree-covered mountains of Nepal. Scattered clouds surrounded the capital city of Kathmandu. The jet banked to the right and then straightened out, settling onto the airstrip.

When we walked outside the international airport, we felt the cool, crisp air of the nearby mountains. A funeral procession with mourners and professional weepers paraded by us. The body, wrapped in a bright orange cloth, lay on a platform held over the pallbearers' heads. We stood to the side, quiet and respectful, and watched them pass. They were on the way to the public pyre where the body would be placed on a wood structure, burned, and pushed into the Bagmati River.

We returned to the airport and boarded a small two-engine prop plane that took us to the pick-up spot for Tiger Tops Jungle Lodge. Before we landed, our plane swept across a large field, driving grazing cattle away from the runway. Finally, we touched down to the hoots and hollers of thirty or so natives as the plane settled onto the grass airstrip.

The local women in either baggy pants or wrapped skirts had tied square baskets to one side of their waists. I watched them walk the cow field, picking up dried dung and dropping it into their reed baskets. They used the manure to fuel their cooking fires and to warm their huts at night.

Once the plane's front door opened, I undid my seatbelt and stood up.

"Look outside! They have elephants waiting for us," I exclaimed to Ron.

Local men with brown skin and high cheek bones wore shin-length skirts tied at the front. They rolled a wooden staircase to the plane's door and held it steady while the passengers descended.

From the staircase Ron and I walked a few feet to a small ladder that leaned against the side of a kneeling elephant. Its stomach was on the ground with its front legs stretched forward and its hind legs bent backwards. The mahout, or trainer, sat on the elephant's neck and kept the animal still. We climbed onto a padded platform and leaned over the wooden guard rail circling the top.

Once Ron and I settled at the front corners with our legs on each side of a vertical post, the mahout instructed the elephant to rise, and we were off. We swayed and jerked to the animal's rhythmic movements as we crossed the field and entered the jungle. Another elephant followed with two other couples. A third elephant trailed and carried hotel supplies, luggage, and liquor.

It took two hours to reach Tiger Tops. We meandered through thick grass, at least three feet above our heads. Along the way our group spooked a couple of wart hogs and saw peacocks, cranes, and gold-striped ducks. We were totally enthralled with the journey, experiencing yet another fantastic venture.

Our traveling band crossed a swift river, and we watched the elephants turn to face the current, walking sideways toward the opposite shore, the white water splashing up to our feet. Once on the other side, we again moved into high grasses. Due to the constant juggling of the elephant, I suddenly felt motion sickness. With little warning I vomited over the side. How embarrassing. If I had known that in five minutes we would arrive at the lodge, I'm sure I could have forced my stomach to stay calm.

Our elephant walked between twelve-foot high bamboo stilts below the raised floor of the guest quarters and stopped. A khaki-uniformed employee held out his hand and assisted us from the padded platform. He escorted us to our accommodations, a large room made of vertical bamboo pole walls, tightly woven with twine. Carafes of water and lanterns rested on side tables, and a bathroom adjoined the bedroom.

Only cold water ran in the guest bathrooms. Early each morning, employees brought hot water in a plastic bucket to our individual rooms. We mixed the almost boiling water with cold water from the tap to wash our bodies as we squatted in the shower.

Tiger Tops Jungle Lodge

Ron noticed a six-foot snake skin stuck to one of the bamboo poles in our bedroom. I wondered if a previous guest had been present when the snake slithered up the wall and shed his skin. We left the skin where it was and speculated about the next guest's reaction. No way was I going to touch it, and Ron thought it was funny to have someone else be surprised by the large skin.

We joined six other lodgers the following morning for three hours of elephant trekking. Each couple mounted an elephant from the raised platform of the guest lodge. As before, the elephants walked between the poles that held up the bamboo building. We boarded our elephant and went into the bush, keeping quiet so as not to scare away wild animals. Within minutes we were ambling through thick, high grass.

All of a sudden, we saw a rhinoceros and he spotted us. As the four elephants surrounded him, he charged us, veered to the right, and raced out of the circle. We rushed after him, cutting through the blinding grass, trying to corral him again. Running up and down marshy levels, swishing through seemingly impenetrable weeds, we gripped the railings and chased after him. Our elephant ran over the rough terrain as we dashed through the swampy jungle, hanging on for dear life. We were cowboys on a larger-than-life round-up. The rhino's grey hide merged into the misty morning, and we soon lost sight of him.

Because male Asian elephants are too unpredictable, Tiger Tops used only female elephants to carry their guests. Every once in a while our particular elephant didn't obey his mahout, so he thumped her head with a heavy broad stick on the backside of an axe. The cracking blow sounded through the jungle, and we winced from the assumed pain. The elephant ambled on with little notice of the chastising. Occasionally she would protest with a soft snort from her trunk or an obvious sway of her head.

We returned for a late supper in the dining room, a circular structure with a thatched roof and a central fireplace. No electricity existed at the jungle lodge; lanterns and candles lit the dining facility and our bedrooms. None of the guests missed the modern conveniences. We all seemed to like the simple jungle experience.

That night we met Janet and Fred Sargent, an older couple from Minnesota. Fred was a retired pediatrician, and the two of them took a special interest in us and the stories of Bahnoo and her struggles to live. They were animal lovers, and they adored babies of all types.

Fred and Janet were also taking an extensive trip around the world. However, they were going first-class and mentioned some of the affluent accommodations they had enjoyed. We told them we were on a shoe-string budget but were lucky enough to have met Jill and David Laylin in Iran.

"Once we knew Ron's graduation date, we started saving," I said. "All extra pennies were put in the travel fund."

"Every six weeks, Bobbi and I sold our blood to the Berkeley Blood Bank," Ron added. "A few days before our flight to Nairobi, our cars and most of our belongings went on sale. But, if we were to stay in Iran for four months, we had to have jobs."

"We're living with a young couple in Tehran. Why don't you visit us?" I asked.

They agreed and decided to change their itinerary to include Iran. Little did we know that we had made lifelong friends from this chance encounter.

We awoke the next morning to a thick fog hanging over the nearby river. We boarded our elephants and began another day of searching for wild animals. The four elephants separated; each mahout looking for more game. As our elephant came to a clearing, we saw the rear of a rhinoceros next to a large tree. We watched for a few minutes until it turned its head and stared at us. Underneath the male was a female rhinoceros. Rhinos mate once every three years. We felt extremely fortunate to be witnesses. My immediate reaction was to capture the event on film and swiveled to take as many shots as possible.

When the female noticed our presence, she rushed from under the male, giving out a high-pitched squeal as she ran into the bush. The male ran in the opposite direction, snorting in apparent disapproval.

On our return to Tiger Tops, we passed two elephants transporting natives with village supplies. Instead of cars or bicycles, everyone walked or rode elephants, the Nepalese jungle taxi.

One night we were awakened by the sound of a bell, alerting us that a tiger was near the lodge's lookout area. Ron and I joined four other guests in a Land Rover for a fifteen-minute drive. We quietly left the vehicle and crept to an enclosed elevated facility, escorted by armed guards. Below us and tied to a stake, was a goat bleating his discomfort. Although we stayed for almost an hour, no tiger came toward the bait.

The following afternoon Ron and I fished the crocodile-infested Rapti River. Tiger Top employees took a rubber raft across the wide river to a sandy island, a perfect spot for casting without catching our fishing flies in overhead trees. As we crossed, I heard a hissing sound. Air was leaking from the rubber raft. We were still in the middle of the river, and the center of the raft was sagging. I panicked, and by using hand motions, I suggested that the natives paddle faster. They laughed at my concern and continued their slow rowing. We made it to the other side, and I jumped out. My feet barely touched the hard sand before I raced to higher ground.

While Ron fished for mahseer, I photographed and wrote in my journal. On one side of me, about fifty feet away, a few crocodiles lay on the beach. On the other side about the same distance away, stood ten vultures waiting in anticipation. They were three-foot tall, bare-headed birds of prey, and they fed on dead carcasses.

Ron caught a few mahseer, a silver carp-like fish with glimmering yellow diagonal designs across its back. To catch a mahseer on a fly was unusual in the seventies. Ron tossed the mahseer back into the water once he removed the hook and fly. There was no way he was going to bend over the water and slowly release the fish. Not with man-eating crocodiles in the river.

After writing my previous day's activity, I put the pen away and closed my journal. As Ron and I fished, casting from high on the sand island, a few hundred cattle were herded illegally across the river and into the national park. Whenever the wet season ended, the natives guided their cattle into the preserve. To discourage such activity, Tiger Top employees moved into the bush and captured the lead cow. They removed its bell and scattered the herd. Since the cows could no longer follow the sound of the bell, they became lost in the thick jungle, and the natives' cattle and subsequent income vanished.

The next day we met Marjorie Silk, wife of renowned *Time/Life* photographer George Silk. She had taken an elephant taxi from deep in the jungle to Tiger Tops lodge. As she came into camp, she sat on the padded platform, holding a dark umbrella above her head, shading her from the hot sun. She told us about her six-hour journey and about passing under a huge tree branch above the trail. Once beyond the large limb, she turned and noticed an enormous python, maybe twenty feet long, lying on the branch. Luckily, the elephant was too large for the python to digest, but the mahout and Marjorie would have made a perfect meal. The snake stayed in place, and they continued their trek into camp.

# Chapter Thirteen
## Customs

On our way back to Iran, Ron and I had a four-hour delay in Kathmandu. To kill time, we shopped and bought lamps for Jill and Christmas gifts for our family in the States.

Hashish was legal in Nepal, and numerous vendors lined the main street in their wood stalls, reminding me of Lucy selling advice in *Peanuts* comic strips. As a surprise holiday present, we purchased a little hashish for our engineering friends in Tehran. The merchant charged us five dollars for a 35-millimeter, film canister stuffed with the intoxicating weed. We bought four canisters and placed them inside my metal fishing rod case.

We changed planes in New Delhi on our way to Iran and went through a brief customs inspection. From the smoldering heat of India, we arrived in Tehran to an early winter snowstorm. Because this was our final destination, Ron and I underwent an intense and thorough custom search. They were looking for weapons and hashish.

Since the hallucinogenic weed was legal in Nepal, I never attempted to hide the film canisters. They were at the top of my rod case. You could see them as soon as you unscrewed the lid. We didn't own guns so that was not a problem.

"Jail time and the amputation of the right hand." Those were the brutal words I heard over the loud speaker.

"What the hell did that mean?" I thought.

In front of us stood an Iranian customs official who explained the announcement to Ron and me.

"Hashish is legal in Nepal. It is not in Iran," he said as he stared directly into my eyes. "The penalty for any possession of hash is many years in jail. And the smuggler's right hand is cut off."

I opened my suitcase on the wooden bench as the words continued to bellow from the loud speaker. I couldn't believe it. At no time did Ron and I realize we could not bring hashish into Iran. How innocent we were.

"What's in there?" the official asked as he pointed to the silver metal tube I had placed on the customs platform.

"A fishing rod," I answered as calmly as possible.

"What else?" he demanded as he glared at me, his dark eyes the color of black olives.

"Only a cotton sleeve," I answered, not sure if my direct comment was acceptable or not.

"What do you mean by 'sleeve'? Is there a shirt in there?" he shouted as he continued to interrogate me.

"No. It's a flannel cloth that protects the fishing rod."

I glanced up at him as he stared fiercely down at me. He must have been standing on a platform because he seemed to tower over me.

I stood still, glancing over his shoulder at the smudged wall behind him, and imagined a prison guard grabbing me.

In my mind I saw the ax swing down on my wrist, my right hand falling to the floor, and my bloody arm stump being seared by hot coals. I was terrified and hoped the customs official had not noticed the shiny perspiration now forming on my forehead.

Finally, he waved his hand, and I moved to the side. He continued to go through the rest of my belongings. He next checked my camera bag, filled with lenses and rolls of film. He opened all the canisters and tossed the ones labeled "Iran" into a wastebasket.

Not wanting to instigate further interrogation, I didn't protest the loss of Bahnoo's puppy photos. I just stood there, trying to project an air of calmness. In reality, I was scared to death. In spite of the cold winter air, sweat soaked my underarms and trickled down my back.

He signaled for me to move on and never said another word. Ron remained beside me and smiled as if going through a brutal customs inspection were a normal occurrence.

How stupid of me. I didn't even smoke cigarettes, let alone hashish. I took an enormous risk, smuggling the intoxicating weed into a foreign country — a country where one is considered guilty until proven innocent, just the opposite of the United States. Besides being forced to live in a filthy jail with criminals and rapists, I would have had my right hand chopped off.

If a Muslim's hand were severed, he could no longer dine with his family or friends. Strict Muslims eat with their right hands out of a communal bowl; they don't employ utensils. Since most homes in Iran did not have toilet paper, the left hand was used to wash their private parts in the bathroom. Having only one hand meant resorting to cleaning and eating with the same hand. Consequently, the disfigured Muslim would never be allowed to participate in any shared meals.

Once we left the confines of the customs area and walked from the Tehran airport, snow covered our coats, and I shivered from the earlier confrontation as well as the cold weather. Ron flagged down a taxi and with hand signals directed the driver to the Laylin villa. Sheets of snow pelted the windshield as we drove through the late night streets. House lights had been turned off, and the city looked like a ghost town.

Ron and I hugged Jill and David in the entrance foyer and followed Ali Akbar as he carried our luggage to the bedroom. We later sat in the living room, telling stories of our trip, and Ali Akbar left to bring in Bahnoo. While traveling these past two weeks, Jill had taken good care of her. She had grown some but still had that wonderful smell of a nursing puppy.

We learned that Bahnoo now slept through the night and was already housebroken.

A week later Ron and I were on the living room floor, playing with the puppies. They were eight weeks old and crawling all over us. Their bodies were just barely beginning to fill out the baggy wrinkles of their oversized black coats.

While we were gone, David and Jill had begun teaching the puppies basic commands. They learned to sit, stay, and come. The Laylins used the word "charge" for "lie down," an Old English hunting command. I continued with Bahnoo's lessons; she was an excellent student — so eager to please.

Before leaving the living room and returning to our bedroom, I stared into the night with Bahnoo at my feet. She followed me everywhere, apparently afraid of losing me again. From the outside lights around the compound, I saw the snow falling, its direction changing at every gust of wind. The family servants lived in small rooms in separate dwellings set apart at the back of the garden beyond the pond.

Bahnoo trailed me into our bedroom, falling onto my heels as I walked down the corridor. I placed her in the middle of the bed with Ron, and from then on she slept with us.

We heard her soft humming as she fell asleep, nestled on top of a thick down comforter that covered our bed.

# Chapter Fourteen
# Teaching Commands

If we had a snow-free day, I took Bahnoo to the outside enclosure and gave her with a few basic commands. She was a fast learner, and her reward was a chance to play by retrieving a wood stick. I waved it back and forth in front of her face, and her head followed its every movement. Her eyes never left the shaking trophy.

"Bahnoo," I shouted once the stick had landed about thirty feet in front of her. David taught me to use her name as the command to fetch.

"If you have more than one dog in a duck blind," he said, "you want only the dog whose name is called to be the one to retrieve the bird."

It didn't take Bahnoo long to run as soon as I called her name. However, if there were more puppies outside, she would join in the melee to retrieve the stick.

Sit, stay, come, and charge were the other commands I reinforced. She loved my undivided attention and the resulting reward.

After twenty minutes of lessons, I brought Bahnoo back into the house and gave her Ali Akbar's special food. When I put the metal bowl on the kitchen floor, she devoured the meal, nearly choking in the process. I watched as saliva studded her muzzle like little pearl beads. No longer did I need to worry about her eating issues.

In another few days, Ron and I welcomed Janet and Fred Sargent to Tehran. Their travel agent had wired Iran Safaris about their arrival dates, and we were happy to see them again.

Once the introductions were over, Jill ushered them into the living room, and David poured them drinks as they sat on the cracked leather sofa. Ali Akbar brought in Sable and Boots, eight puppies and popcorn. The six of us told stories of Nepal, laughing at our adventures while we threw buttered popcorn to the dogs.

"Let me see Bahnoo," Fred said.

He specifically wanted to check on her now that he was in Iran. I picked Bahnoo up and placed her on his lap. He bent over and put his ear to the squirming puppy's chest and listened to her heart. He also rubbed her body, concentrating on her shoulders and hips.

"Make sure you get some x-rays," he said. She has some major deformities. Vets in the States might be able to help."

I was saddened by his remark but was determined to persevere. "We'll be together for many years to come," I thought.

"Let me hold her," Janet requested as she reached over and took the puppy from Fred's lap. Bahnoo immediately jumped up on her hind legs and licked Janet's face, twisting in a circle above her knees.

"You certainly don't have to worry about her energy. She's got plenty," Janet said as she stroked Bahnoo's back.

Soon the puppy settled down, and we went back to telling stories of our collective international adventures. When their taxi arrived in the gathering darkness, we said our 'good-byes' and walked out into the brisk winter air. Plans were made for sightseeing the following day, and Ron and I thanked them again for coming to see us in Iran.

# Chapter Fifteen
# Hashish

The next day Janet, Fred, and I visited the national museum and went shopping. They were surprised at the great expense of everyday items such as toasters and lamps, but appreciated the cost of ceramics and brass, as well as the skills of the local miniature artists. Their flight to the Orient the following evening meant our time together was way too short.

"We'll see you in Minnesota," I said as I hugged them at their hotel entrance. "We had another fabulous time together — Nepal and now Iran. Thanks so much for visiting us and checking out Bahnoo. I really appreciate it."

Ron had to leave that morning for the Persian Gulf and missed the day's adventure with the Sargents. As a consultant for Iran's Department of the Protection to the Environment, he checked specific oil spills and suggested clean-up procedures for its polluted waters.

When Ron returned to Tehran later that week, we challenged ourselves to explore different areas without Jill or David as our guides. We wanted to learn more about Iran's culture and expand our horizons in this restrictive country.

One day we ventured into the Grand Bazaar, shielding ourselves from the brisk winter weather. As we walked along the narrow pathway between merchant stalls, a few oncoming men banged into me, hissing at me. Ron wrapped a protective arm around my shoulders and pulled me close. The fanatical men finally left me alone.

Iran was a male-dominated country as most of the inhabitants were Muslim. Women were considered second-class citizens. However, under the Shah's guidance women were allowed to wear Western clothes and even encouraged to attend colleges, not just in Iran but in France, England, and the United States. Most of the time I felt safe; however, if I were ever alone with the rural men or religious extremists, I sensed a threatening presence.

Once outside the bazaar, I noticed how striking the Muslim women of Tehran were. They paid an unusual amount of attention to their appearance. If they wore the chador, their extensive make-up, fashionable purses, and expensive shoes were stunning. All that showed outside the confines of the chador were elaborate accessories. Most of these women grasped the chador under their chins; a few actually held the all-consuming cloth in place by biting it, leaving both hands free to shop.

The city men were handsome with olive skin and thick, straight black hair. The rural Iranian men, however, had dark skin, thick mustaches, and short heavy bodies. Their work as outdoor employees made them appear strong but coarse and less appealing.

As Ron and I walked through the central shopping area of Tehran, we noticed that street merchants wrapped their heads in wool scarves, keeping warm from the cold mountain air. They squatted on their heels, leaning next to buildings, and called out to passing people, asking them to buy their products. We watched them as they smoked and drank coffee while selling cigarettes, candy, and newspapers on the crowded city sidewalks.

Whenever we wondered around the shopping zone, I was surprised by the smell of open sewers on each side of the busy road. There were no guardrails, and cars kept falling into the deep ditches. At every street corner, Ron and I jumped over the filthy stream. Even in winter, we saw rats trying to capture any edible garbage flowing down the sewer.

Snow began to fall, and we returned home. Jill had asked Ali Akbar to put up the Christmas tree David had bought earlier in the week. The sweet scent of sap filled the air as we entered the living room. The four of us decorated the tree with glass ornaments, listened to holiday records, and watched spitting flames in the fireplace.

A few days later, Ron and I invited some American friends to join us at the Laylin compound. We decided to try some of the hashish that I had risked losing my hand over. Since I didn't smoke, I proposed putting the grass in brownies. However, the only brownies I had ever made came from a box, and boxed food was not available in Iran.

"We'll go to the bazaar to pick up the ingredients," suggested Jill.

Once at the bazaar, we strolled from food stall to food stall. Chocolate in one area, flour in another, eggs in another, sugar in still another, and butter in the last stall. No supermarkets existed, and we shopped the way most Iranians did in the early seventies.

"I have vanilla at home," Jill said. "I bought it when I was last in England."

Back in their kitchen with the puppies yipping from their wood enclosure, I attempted to make the brownie recipe. The only thing I remembered was the mixture should heat at 350 degrees for thirty minutes. The ingredient amounts were a complete guess.

"Darn. I'm sorry we can't try the dessert," Jill said. "David just told me we have a business meeting tonight. We can't miss it."

"We'll be home late. Don't wait up," David said as they walked out the front door.

Within an hour we welcomed our engineering friends at the front door. As expatriates, the scientists and their wives enjoyed the special dessert before dinner. With a slightly induced high, we laughed at silly jokes, watched red flames burst upward in the fireplace, and saw shadows dance on the walls as we ate a delicious dinner by Ali Akbar. Our taste buds were besieged with lamb, eggplant, onions, and spices. It was one of the best meals I had ever tasted.

We returned to the living room and laughed until our sides hurt. The puppies bounded out from the kitchen, tails thrashing against the chair legs as they rushed to greet us. Bahnoo trailed behind and headed straight for me, jumping into my lap. Her baby-sharp teeth were now rounded white buds. Typical of a Lab, her jaws were strong but extremely gentle, perfect for retrieving ducks without mangling the edible parts.

After saying "Goodnight" to our friends who were returning to the States the following week, we helped Ali Akbar clean the remnants of a fun party and shuffled back to the bedroom. Bahnoo followed, padding down the long hallway, her little legs scrambling over the tiles trying to keep up.

# Chapter Sixteen

# Holidays

In winter Muslims celebrate the birth of Muhammad, the Prophet of Islam who was born during the seventh century in Mecca, Saudi Arabia. Following his death, there was a separation within the Muslim religion over his successor. However, during the snowy holiday, Shiite and Sunni branches of Islam join together in their following of Muhammad. Colored lights blazed across the streets and around building windows, reminding me of our Christmas celebrations back home.

Winter winds swept down from the mountains, and snow fell throughout January. During the day, Bahnoo slept on a Persian carpet in the living room, the sun bathing over her. The cold air was kept at bay while she lay with her front and back legs stretched outward. She looked like a stuffed toy, spread like an eagle over the thick carpet, softly snoring as she lay sound asleep.

Outside the snow blew in drifts, and icy roads intensified the number of accidents. I heard sirens in the distance whenever I cracked open the massive front door. As the afternoon sky darkened, Bahnoo turned over and napped with her head on her crossed front paws. I wrote in my journal, read books, and waited for Jill and David to arrive home.

Snow continued to fall throughout the month. Nevertheless, I still had to work periodically at the office downtown. One night after the staff had left the building, I typed urgently needed letters while smelling scorched coffee and stale cigarettes. I asked the tea boy, who was actually a tribal man in his fifties, to call a cab for me. The word 'taxi' is the same in Farsi as English.

He understood the telephone book but had never used a telephone. He stared at the black contraption, not sure what he should do. He first dialed the number with the receiver still in its cradle. I demonstrated the calling procedure by lifting the handle before dialing. He followed my hand instructions, but as soon as he heard a dial tone, he began talking. I took the phone from his grip and dialed the number. Once I heard someone talking, I gave him the receiver. He looked at me, his eyes the color of old pennies, and spoke into the handle. Surprised by the talking handset, he smiled at his accomplishment and bowed slightly toward me as he returned to clean the offices. He seemed pleased by his success and left with a huge grin across his face. Within a few minutes an orange taxi arrived, and I departed for home.

The following day Jill had her driver take Bahnoo and me to the Iran Safaris veterinarian.

"Let's see what we have here," Dr. Hamidi said as he placed Bahnoo on the examination table.

"We'll need x-rays to see how extensive her defects are," he said as he moved his hand slowly over the three-month-old puppy.

After putting a stethoscope to her chest, he declared, "She has a heart murmur. And I can tell she has some bone distortions."

He asked Jill and me to hold Bahnoo's legs, and he placed her belly-up on the covered table. He took x-rays while Jill and I held her. We didn't wear protective gear during the process, not knowing any better. The pictures showed that she had a slight curvature of the spine, her left elbow and shoulder were incorrectly formed, and neither hip socket had developed properly. One hip was only partially encased; the other was not at all. Her strong muscles held the legs in her partially-formed hip sockets.

Dr. Hamidi sent the x-rays to my veterinarian in California, explaining the need for a quick response so I could comply with U.S. immigration rules. Dr. Roger wrote back immediately.

"She'll never live past two," he declared in his letter. "With all her health issues she doesn't have much of a chance. Have Bobbi bring her in when she returns to town, and we'll see what we can do."

Silently I renewed my vow to Bahnoo, promising to send her back to the States. "Yes," I declared. "She will be with me for the rest of her life, no matter how long or short it is."

# Chapter Seventeen
# A Night Out

The next day Ron and I decided to take an orange taxi to meet Jill and David for dinner. An icy wind blew from the mountains as we trudged through the snow and slush to the main road.

Taxi rates were low in Tehran because cab drivers picked up other passengers along the way. A potential rider stood on the sidewalk and yelled his destination through the taxi's open window. If the cab were going the same way, he'd stop and pick up the passenger. If not, the cab kept on moving. Consequently, the taxi drivers maneuvered in and out of traffic and tipped their bodies outward to hear the potential passenger's destination, steering with only their left hand.

As Ron and I scrambled into the cab, I surveyed the five men and one chador-covered woman crammed into the vehicle. I sat on Ron's lap and we drove off. Taking an Iranian taxi was like catching a cheap carnival ride; you never knew exactly what was going to happen. Up, down, sideways, and backwards. The one we flagged, stuffed with a half dozen Iranians, weaved through traffic at full speed, and then the driver slammed on his brakes, sliding on ice around a sharp curve. During the ride, he yelled indiscernible swear words at other drivers as he leaned on his horn. It was always a thrill whenever one rode in a taxi — orange or not.

At the fancy downtown restaurant we sat on padded chairs around a decorated table draped with white linens. We unfolded our napkins and looked at the menu. Crystal chandeliers hung from the ceiling, and mirrors adorned the walls. Silverware framed the plates with a dessert fork and spoon placed across the top. Although the atmosphere seemed European, the menu was definitely Iranian.

I bent forward listening intently to the waiter reciting the specials for the evening. He was a handsome man, taller than most small-statured Iranian men. However, he had a heavy accent, and it was hard for me to discern his descriptions. Finally, David interpreted the menu.

"Try this," he said pointing to a specific dish on the English menu. "You'll like the meat and fruit combination."

"I'm just going to have a salad," said Jill. "It'll have enough goodies to be filling. You should try the dish David suggested. I've had it before. It's super."

When my dinner arrived, it consisted of plums, apricots, fresh herbs, and diced chicken on top of rice. The sauce of white wine and butter completed the entree. Jill was right. It was excellent.

"My mother is Greek," Ron said. "I'm going to have the stuffed grape leaves. We'll see how close it comes to my mom's recipe." He had grape leaves packed with ground lamb and rice. Yes. It was similar to those dinners his mother made. However, he noted, "Not quite as good."

David had rack of lamb, some greens, and eggplant. "The eggplant is considered the potato of Iran," he explained. "And lamb is perfect here."

The waiter brought cocktails to the table and later delivered wine and coffee for Jill and David. After dinner she lit a cigarette, blowing the smoke upward, and looked at me over the rim of her cup.

"I think Bahnoo is out of the woods. What do you think?" asked Jill.

"Yes. I agree."

"Let's take her back to the vet's. We'll get her paperwork and the last of her shots."

"That's perfect. She'll then be set for her flight to the States."

The half dozen dessert choices were of French origin. The four of us decided to share a crème brulee and another glass of wine before heading home. As the waiter removed the last of the dishes, we remarked about the continental atmosphere and excellent cuisine. Ron and I noted that Tehran was definitely a city of contrasts — from the rural ethnic groups to the educated elitists.

# Chapter Eighteen
# Bandar Abbas

When Ron traveled outside Tehran, I kept Bahnoo with me during the night. Our suite was at the far end of the house, and I was in the middle of reading *The Exorcist*. I switched on the bedside light and opened my book. It wasn't long before I thought I heard strange noises — footsteps and whispering coming from outside the bedroom. My hair stood up on my neck, and I slipped out of bed as quietly as possible and closed the room door.

It was past midnight when I fell into a restless sleep, filled with nightmares. I cradled Bahnoo beside me and rubbed her thick black fur until I finally dropped into a deep sleep. I wanted to see Ron. He had been gone over a week, way too long.

Two days later I flew six hundred miles south to Bandar Abbas, a port city on the Persian Gulf. The Shah had expanded it into a major trade center, and Ron was working in the area. When I arrived, I learned I could not travel to the military base because there were no facilities for women. Instead of immediately returning to Tehran, I decided to stay for a few days of fishing and swimming.

After checking into the beach front Gameroon Hotel, I walked outside and immediately noticed the women. Not only did they wear the bulky chadors in the heat of the day, but they also wore ugly face masks. The black material covered the top half of their faces and had sharp, pointed noses and tiny eye holes. They each looked like the wicked witch in *The Wizard of Oz*, scary and hideous.

Hundreds of years ago when fishermen from other tribes came to their shores, they captured and raped the women. Once they started wearing the repulsive face masks, the men were frightened and left the women alone. The centuries-old tradition continued until modern times.

While walking along the sand road, I saw several children run between the nearby stucco houses. The young girls with their hair flowing down their backs were wearing pretty, colorful dresses. However, they also wore the ugly face masks.

I returned to the hotel just as a sandstorm hit. The lobby was filled with powdery dust — so tiny and light it saturated the air. I could barely see to the end of the hallway. A fine cloud of dust settled on my clothes, hair, and suitcase. In the haze of my room, I changed to a bathing suit and robe and left the hotel.

When I walked on the grass on the way to the beach, puffs of dust emerged from around my sandals. It became hard to breathe, and I covered my nose and mouth with the end of my towel. Finally the wind stopped.

The white beach was practically empty as far as I could see in both directions. Seaweed lay in dark clumps on the gorgeous sand, and I could smell and even taste, the salt air. My toes squeaked on the hot beach as I raced from my towel to the cooling ocean waves. The wet sand felt crisp beneath my feet as I walked head down, looking at interesting shells tangled in the seaweed along the shore.

Out in the bright turquoise water three women, wearing their black chadors and face masks, waded into the sea. Astonished that they wore their heavy garments and masks into the water, I watched them move past their waists into the white froth of the gentle waves. They chatted and giggled, splashing the surf as they moved among the ripples. They were obviously happy, and I was amazed.

"How could they tolerate their chadors and masks?" I thought as I stood just fifty feet away in a bathing suit. They turned and looked at me, wondering I'm sure, how I could wear such a skimpy outfit in a public place.

# Chapter Nineteen
# Taxi Driver

On my return flight to Tehran, I arrived at night. I scrambled into a waiting orange cab at the airport and gave the driver a piece of paper with the Laylin address written on it. He stared at the scrap of paper, turned, and grinned at me but said nothing.

The dark-skinned man, probably in his forties, smelled of dirty clothes that had probably not been washed in months. His features were indistinct, and I paid no attention to him, surveying the nearby buildings as we drove past the lights of the city.

When we came to the familiar stone wall with glass shards across the top, the driver shut off the motor, looked over his shoulder at me, and again smiled, showing half a dozen missing teeth.

I emerged from the taxi and opened the passenger front door to retrieve my camera gear, tackle bag, and stainless steel rod case. The driver released the trunk, took out my suitcase, and placed it near to the rear wheel of the cab.

As I bent over to gather my belongings which were lying on the front seat, he approached me from behind. Without a word he leaned over me, his hairy forearm mashed into my face.

His mouth was so close to mine, his spray of spit splashed onto my cheek. With his other hand, he gripped the side of the door frame and pressed his pelvis into my backside.

His filthy, smelly body shoved hard against me. He thrust, back and forth, ramming his groin into me.

I fell forward but the metal rod case was jammed between the outside door frames. It kept me from tumbling onto the front seat.

He continued to shove me, pushing his rough hand down on my shoulders. Stumbling off balance, I twisted to the left, and swiveled under his grip.

Black fury roared in my head as I elbowed him with all my might and escaped his grasp.

He lost his hold on me. Fuming I staggered to face him.

"That's not very nice!" I exclaimed, glaring at him with furious anger.

What a ridiculous understatement. I could have been raped, and all I could come up with were those four words. Thank goodness, the metal tube across my chest blocked him from pushing me onto the front seat.

Within seconds, the small door in the wooden drive-through gate opened, and the Laylins' watchman appeared. In a blur of the moment, the taxi vanished into the darkness, leaving me shaken but safe. I fled to the security of the compound, brushing past the watchman as he carried my luggage inside.

"I hate him," I said as pent-up tears streamed down my cheeks.

"What happened?" Jill asked in surprise as she met me in the foyer.

"The taxi driver attacked me," I said stifling a sob. I leaned into her shoulder as she hugged me, wrapping her arms tightly around my shaking body.

"Disgusting," Jill answered with passion. "It happens. I'm glad you're home."

With another warm hug, she urged me down the hall and into my bathroom. I washed my face, scrubbing hard to remove any trace of the driver's spatter.

Jill took my hand and led me into the living room where we settled into comfy chairs angled to face each other by the fireplace. Chilled by the terrifying episode, I stretched my hands over the fire grate. I kept trembling as the image spun through my mind.

My head pounded and crying made it more severe. I continued to shiver, attempting to ward off the evil spirit of the cab driver. Ali Akbar stood at the side, overhearing my conversation and shaking his head with sadness.

"Should I bring in Bahnoo?" he asked.

"Please," answered Jill. "And bring in some ice. I'll make drinks."

The rest of the evening was spent relating my encounter with the taxi driver and learning more about the culture of tribal men.

"Men are kept away from women in many places in the Middle East," Jill explained. "When there's a female by herself, especially a Western woman, the uneducated men believe it's okay to assault or even molest her."

I cuddled Bahnoo to my chest, circling my fingers around her squirming body, as she licked the tears from my face. A couple of glasses of vodka eased my distress, and I actually giggled at my silly response when I said, "That's not very nice."

Thank goodness I could laugh at my stupid comment. I was home with Jill and safe.

# Chapter Twenty
## Caspian Horses

"Want to see some Caspian horses?" asked David a week later. "It's a small horse, standing between nine and eleven hands high. You know a hand is four inches, right?"

"Yes, I know, but I'm not sure Ron does," I said. "I've been riding since I was five, but he's relatively new to horses."

"It's thought to be the oldest known breed in the world, dating back some five thousand years," David said. "My sister raises them at her home out in the country."

"I'm impressed," I said. "Where does she live?"

"A few hours from here. We'll spend the night," he said. "Louise and Narcy love company."

Louise Firouz rediscovered the Caspian horse in the mountain villages north of Tehran a few years earlier. She was an expert equestrian and bred horses at her original home in the Virginia countryside near Washington, D.C. When she saw this particular animal pulling a heavy wagon in Iran, she was curious and wanted to know more about it. The animal was too small to be considered a horse, and yet it didn't have any pony gaits or pony conformations. She arranged to have three Caspian horses trucked to Narcy's estate, thus, beginning her passion for the Caspian breed.

A gas lantern illuminated the front entrance of their beautiful wood and tile villa out in the desert west of Tehran. They had three children, ten dogs, fifty horses, and two house guests. The servants had our rooms ready for the four of us the moment we arrived.

Narcy was related to the former Qajar dynasty, the rulers before the Pahlavis, and he had the title, prince; although, he never used it. He stood in the hallway entrance and greeted us as we appeared at the front door.

Louise, tall and thin with light brown hair, shook our hands and waved us into the living room. Dressed in faded jeans and a plaid wool shirt she looked like a L. L. Bean model.

She had written a thesis on the Caspian horse and was considered to be the person to revive it from extinction.

Their home was warm and welcoming. Lush Persian carpets covered the floor, and gold-framed paintings of horses, bronze statues of horses, and books upon books on horses decorated the interior. To award a few spaces to Narcy, I spotted several works of art revealing his Persian ancestry. The paintings depicted royal or religious themes using actual gold ink. Some were large, but most were quite small. Iranian artists were renowned for their intricate miniatures, and he had acquired quite a few.

Standing with her back to the fire while we told horse stories in the living room, Louise recalled the time she had ridden a large horse on a steep mountain trail. It tripped and tossed her to the ground. She dislocated her shoulder, and people told her to stop riding; she was too old.

"I beg your pardon. The horse fell. I didn't," she told those that had given her the unsolicited advice. We laughed at her statement and remarked that she still continued to ride both in Iran and in the States.

"Come. Look at these paintings," Louise said as she rose and directed me to the library.

We stood alone in the paneled room surrounded by shelves of books and original works of art.

"Did you know I'm sending a Lab puppy back to New York?" I asked. "Her name is Bahnoo."

"Yes. David told me," she said. "I'm so glad they could help. As an animal lover," she added, "I believe dogs and horses have real emotions. Almost human-like. Do you?"

"Yes. Bahnoo seems to sense my every mood. I'm so glad we've saved her. She'll be sent to the East Coast in just a few days."

# Chapter Twenty-One
# Bahnoo's Taxi Ride

After our lengthy stay in Iran, Ron and I were ready to leave. We had numerous errands to run before departing Tehran for New Zealand. I remembered my conversation with David a month earlier.

'"We don't have pets," he had said. "We have only working dogs, and she's not healthy enough to be one." He added, "One of our workers will drown her in the pond."

"No," I said. "Let me send her back to the States."'

Since that conversation, I had complied with all the American immigration policies. Later that day, I would obtain the Iranian veterinarian's paperwork. With the Laylins' help, Bahnoo would travel to New York where she would be held in quarantine for twenty-four hours. Then my parents would collect her and keep her at their home for two months.

From New Zealand Ron and I would fly to the East Coast and pick up Bahnoo at my parents' home in Connecticut. We had summer jobs lined up in Vermont and would later drive cross country to our cottage in California.

To help facilitate Bahnoo's journey, David asked an employee to make a sturdy container made of wood boards. Plastic travel kennels had not yet been invented.

As I stood in the garden area, overseeing the crate's construction, I heard the clip-clop of hooves on the street. Peeking through the narrow door in the entrance gate, I saw a horse-drawn wagon piled high with garbage. The driver was encouraging the struggling horse up the hill. He was using his voice and not a whip. I was pleased to see such a compassionate man, one who did not have much of his own yet was kind to his working animal.

When Ron gave his report on pollution control to the Iranian government, I picked up Bahnoo's immigration paperwork. The veterinarian gave Bahnoo her last vaccinations and final inspection. He then instructed me about her medicines and about the long flight she would endure to the States.

"Give her half the dosage." he said as he handed me four pills. "And we'll change the paperwork to reflect only *Bahnoo* as her name. If I write her full name, Shah Bahnoo Siya, the Iranian inspectors will consider it an insult to the Shah's wife."

He added, "They might even kill your dog because her name would be such an offense to the royal family."

That evening the four of us sat in the living room, enjoying cocktails and telling stories. We stared at the flames in the fireplace, and watched puppy shadows flickering on the walls. Our laughter echoed through the room as we recalled the many adventures we had during our four months together.

I reached down and picked up Bahnoo from the tangle of black puppies. She looked up at me with her big eyes, revealing her absolute devotion. This would be our last night in Iran, and I savored every moment with Bahnoo and the Laylins.

Before Jill and David left for work, they arranged for a taxi to take Bahnoo and me to the airport. Inside the Laylin compound, the cab driver screamed, "Saag. Saag," furious to see me put a dog inside his cab. He would not carry us. When Ali Akbar heard the noise, he came out of the house and convinced the driver to take me as well as the puppy to the airport.

Strict Muslims believed dogs were unclean and that people should not have pets. They were not even allowed to touch a dog. There was no way he wanted Bahnoo inside his cab. Maybe in the trunk, but never inside his taxi.

"You'll get more money," Ali Akbar pleaded in Farsi for Bahnoo to ride inside. The driver continued to shout, "Na," shaking his head "no." Once he saw the rials roll off Ali Akbar's fingers, he relented and let Bahnoo ride with me inside the cab. The men latched the crate to the rear of the taxi and tied the trunk lid to broken parts of the fender and bumper.

A few minutes before the taxi arrived, I had fed Bahnoo the prescribed medicine and washed it down with a squirt of water. The medicine was to help her rest during the nineteen-hour trip to the Kennedy International Airport. However, I misunderstood the vet's instructions.

He said, "Half the dosage."

Because of Bahnoo's long flight hours, I thought he said, "Double the dosage."

Consequently, I gave her four times what she was supposed to consume. During the cab ride to the international airport, I held her on my lap, surprised to see her so drugged. Her eye lids grew heavy, and she became groggy, and soon unconscious.

The cabdriver roared off with a great show of speed as he raced onto the airport highway. As we flew past vehicles and desert bushes, she began to eliminate her waste.

"No! No!" I screamed as the warm liquid filled my skirt.

The driver turned at the noise and smelled the putrid waste. Jerking the taxi to the right and jumping the curb, he slammed on the brakes. Once the taxi stopped, he shot from the car and raced around to yank open my door. Yelling at me in Farsi, he pulled me outside.

I held up my skirt, keeping the lifeless puppy in my lap. As soon as we reached the grass, I rested her on the narrow strip of green and flipped the muck off my skirt.

The driver continued to roar, his arms waving in the air. At least he didn't leave me on the side of the highway. He could have done that. I'm not sure anyone would have picked me up — anyone, that is, with good intentions.

I used the towel from the crate and wiped off my dress while Bahnoo lay motionless on the grass. The driver let us return to his vehicle, probably expecting more money. He hunched forward and bellowed at me the whole way to the airport. I never looked at him but continued to clean the mess clinging to Bahnoo's fur. I whispered soothing words to her as we rushed down the highway, the driver raising his fist and screaming, "Na. Na," steering with just one hand.

Finally we arrived at the international airport. I hired a porter to take the crate to the appropriate counter and followed him, carrying Bahnoo in the dirty towel. Once at the ticket counter, I pressed my cheek to Bahnoo's face as I slid her into the crate.

Tears filled my eyes when I realized she still could not stand. Her legs flopped out behind her. The Iranian workers thought I was sending a dead dog back to the States. They didn't care. As long as I gave them money, and the dog was leaving their country, they didn't care one bit.

"I killed her," I thought.

I choked back sobs and wrapped my arms around my waist as the airline handlers whisked the crate onto a small truck. Luggage, supplies, and a few animal containers were being transported to the belly of the plane. I had a terrible fear of losing Bahnoo after months of trying to save her.

She was booked on a KLM flight with a stopover at the famous animal hotel in Amsterdam. She would be fed, watered, and walked during the two-hour layover.

The original cab driver left as soon as he was paid, and I flagged down another orange taxi. What a tragedy. I had actually overdosed Bahnoo.

"Would she survive her flight?" I thought. "Would her health be further damaged?"

I wiped tears from my face and slowly regained my composure while riding in the taxi. In another few days, Ron and I would be fly fishing in New Zealand.

Bahnoo was a fighter. She would survive.

# Chapter Twenty-Two
## Stateside

Ron and I finished packing and said our heartfelt "Good-byes" to Jill and David. We returned to the Tehran airport by taxi, passing our neighborhood and reliving some of our more exciting adventures in Iran.

I never did buy a Persian carpet, but instead, I rescued a Labrador retriever. Or I hoped I did. At this point in time, I didn't know if she had survived her drug-induced journey from Tehran to New York City.

After a week in Christchurch, I received a detailed letter from my mother in Connecticut.

"Bahnoo spent twenty-four hours in quarantine and is now home," she wrote. "I picked her up at the airport last week. She smelled awful and slept two whole days. But now she's up and running about. She's the smartest, most loving puppy ever." Spoken like a true grandmother.

My mother also relayed the animal walker's note that had been scribbled on Bahnoo's ticket. "Your dog slept during her time in Amsterdam and never woke up."

Two months after we had received my mom's letter, my father collected Ron and me at the New York airport and drove us to Connecticut. It was an hour's drive, and we chatted nonstop about our latest adventures in New Zealand. My dad couldn't wait for us to see Bahnoo. He was so proud of her.

"You won't believe how she's grown," he said. "She's a wonderful dog, and if you want to leave her with us, that's okay."

As we stopped in the driveway before going into the garage, my mother opened the screened porch door. Bahnoo recognized us as soon as we called her name and scampered to greet us. She raced up and down the stone walk, peeing in her excitement. As she twisted about us, we finally corralled her in our arms. She squealed with delight and leaped up to kiss our faces. So much hugging and hooting that my parents stood to the side, laughing in response.

Finally we settled down, and I gave Bahnoo a few commands to see if she remembered them after not seeing us for two months.

"Sit. Stay. Come." She was perfect. Then I said "Charge," a command my parents would not have known. Ron and I stood speechless as Bahnoo dropped to the 'down' position. She had remembered everything.

We left a week later for three months in New England. Ron had been hired by the Orvis Company, and I by *The Vermont News Guide*, a weekly newspaper in Manchester. The *Fly Fisherman Magazine* was located in the same town; Ron easily worked for both companies.

We lived across a mountain, about twenty minutes away, in a converted barn on the banks of the West River. As a thank-you gift to the Orvis and magazine staffs, we invited a dozen people to our home for hors d'oeuvres, drinks, and a slide show, illustrating different fishing spots we visited on our worldwide journey.

Before we dimmed the living room lights, I noticed that Bahnoo had joined the seated guests as they sipped their wine. She had something in her mouth. Her lips had puffed outward, and she was making a humming noise as she proudly carried her possession. She had slipped outside while the guests were arriving and, being a typical Lab, she was bringing me a present.

"Look what Bahnoo has," I exclaimed as the cheerful company stopped to see what she held. They had already learned her story about being rescued from Iran, and were now gathered in a circle to see what she had.

I bent down and looked around the room, making sure I had everyone's attention. Bahnoo was so proud of her gift that she circled the group, still humming as she moved among the many legs.

"Drop," I commanded with my hand placed in front of her mouth.

Using her tongue, she pushed out the object and into my palm. There sat a slimy green frog, squished and flattened, that she had scraped from the nearby road.

"Eck!" everyone cried in unison.

There was a huge explosion of laughter as I raced to our streamside deck and threw the frog into the river. I immediately washed my hands as I listened to the chatter from our friends. They all had Labs or knew of people who did. Labradors were very popular, and our guests definitely understood the consequences of unsought gifts.

Retrieving was a specialty most Labs did naturally. Bahnoo seemed to be more adept than the average, constantly willing to please and carry presents to me.

When the summer ended, the three of us drove cross country, stopping in Minnesota to visit the Sargents. We learned that they had sold their house and were moving to San Francisco. We would be neighbors and visit regularly for the next twenty years. They even became my financial supporters when I started the Angler's Calendar Company in 1975.

Once we returned to Berkeley, I took Bahnoo to Dr. Roger's veterinarian office.

"She looks good!" he said. "Bring her to me every two months and I'll recheck her joints."

"Great. I'm really pleased. It's been touch and go for so long," I responded with a satisfying smile.

"I'll order a drug that should help with Bahnoo's pain. She'll be in a clinical trial, a science program that researches dog reactions to arthritic medicine. The results might help with human arthritis," Dr. Roger said. "You'll like the program. As long as Bahnoo is involved, she'll have free medicine and vet visits."

What a perfect ending to the challenging rescue of Bahnoo. She was my Shah Bahnoo Siya, my black empress. And she was a fighter.

She lived to be fourteen years old.

# EPILOGUE

Because of Bahnoo, a throw-away puppy who conquered numerous health issues, I also defeated several challenges. I survived breast cancer, heart problems, and divorce.

I had kept my promise to Bahnoo, determined to save her from certain death. She in turn comforted me through my ensuing trials, and brought me joy and happiness all her days.

From Bahnoo there was no anger, no envy — just pure innocence, loyalty, and unconditional love.

**Creative Nonfiction Disclaimer:** All names are factual except for the veterinarians. Recollections are to the best of my knowledge. These stories took place in 1967, 1972, and 1973.To aid in the narrative flow, timelines have been condensed.

Bahnoo waiting for a command

# GLOSSARY

| | |
|---|---|
| Allah Akbar: | God is great. |
| Azan: | Call to prayer. |
| Bahnoo: | Lady. |
| Banu: | Lady (correct spelling). |
| Chador: | A large cloth, usually black, that covers a Muslim woman in Iran from the top of her head to her ankles. Only her face is shown. |
| Enshalla: | God willing. |
| Estacon: | Tiny glass cups, used to sip tea. |
| Hijab: | A scarf worn by Muslim women to cover their hair. |
| Mahout: | Elephant handler. |
| Muchakher: | Thank you. |
| Na: | No. |
| Rial: | The Iranian money unit. |
| Saag: | Dog. Usually used in a negative way. |
| Salom: | Hello. |
| Shah: | King or ruler. |
| Shah Bahnoo Siya: | Black Empress. |
| Siya: | Black. |

Jersey Shore

# 2015 Facts:
# Iran, India, and Nepal

### *Iran:*
Area: Over two times the size of Texas.
Climate: Long hot summers. Cool short winters.
Population: Almost 80 million.
Government: Theocratic.
Religion: Shiite Muslim (90%), Sunni Muslim (7%).
Language: Persian (Farsi).

### *India:*
Area: One third the size of the United States.
Climate: Tropical to very hot and dry to mountainous.
Population: 1.3 billion.
Government: Based on English common and statutory law.
Religion: Hindu (80%), Muslim (15%).
Language: Hindi and English.

### *Nepal:*
Area: About the size of North Carolina.
Climate: Summer, winter, spring, fall, and monsoon.
Population: Over 29 million.
Government: Federal Democratic Republic.
Religion: Hindu (80%), Buddhist (11%), Muslim (5%).
Language: Nepalese.

Loving waters, beaches, and sand

# ACKNOWLEDGEMENTS

*I am indebted to all those who have encouraged and helped me through my years of writing. I couldn't have accomplished my finished books without their support.*

**B & B Support at Book Signings:** Joe and Connie Anderson, Sue Ellen and Rod Coffman, Janet and Marty Downey, Gillian Drummond, Sally and Corky Elliott, Carolyn and Dave Erickson, Marilyn Weir Haber, Jack and Judy Hall, Mary and Bob Herman, Helga Komp Hodge, Kathy Kane, Sue and Tom Moore, Gina and Dan O'Donnell, Debbye and Hunt Oliver, Ginger and Dexter Rogers, Nancy and Doug Strand, Steve and Shari Wassell, Pat Whipkey, Georgina and Don Wolverton.

**Copy Editing:** Pam Strickland. Phone: 865-386-0805. pamstrickland@mac.com. Website: pamstrickland.org.

**Formatting:** Bob Ballard of Working Class Publishing, Stevens Point, Wisconsin.

**Photographs:** Bobbi Phelps Wolverton and Ron Cordes.

**Cover Photo:** Supplied by Shooting Star Photography, North Logan, Utah. Black Labrador cover puppy provided by Puppy Steps Training in Northern Utah.

# ACKNOWLEDGEMENTS
## (Continued):

**Printing:** Worzalla, Stevens Point, Wisconsin.

**Proof Readers:** Virginia Phelps Clemens, Kathy Economy, Carolyn Erickson, Diane Gower, Susan Church Moore, Bill Sport, and Gail Thomasson. Thank you for your thoughtful comments, especially to David Laylin who patiently helped with fifty-year-old details of Iran.

**Title:** Gail Capossela Shiller, Sally Chapman Elliott, Linda Stone Kemp, and Lee Damm Yadrick (dear friends from Darien High School).

**Web Masters:** Lou Miller and Abraham Tol.

**Writing Advice:** Authors Guild of Tennessee, Knoxville Writers Group, Nick Lyons, and Buddy Macatee.

*My special thanks and love to Larry Chapman, my caring partner who improves my life daily. He fixes my electronics, escorts me to book signings, and loves me unconditionally. How very lucky I am.*

*Bobbi*

First day at the Times News,
Twin Falls, Idaho. 1978

Fly Fishing at Henry's Lake, Idaho

# ABOUT THE AUTHOR

Photo by Cinthia D. Stafford

Bobbi Phelps Wolverton grew up in Darien, Connecticut, forty miles from New York City. Following graduation from Pine Manor College and Katharine Gibbs Secretarial School, she was employed as a legal secretary in San Francisco. In 1965 she joined World Airways as an international flight attendant.

In 1967 Bobbi traveled solo around the world and returned to complete her education at the University of California, Berkeley. She then rejoined the charter airline industry, working for Saturn Airways until 1972. She and her then husband traveled internationally for eighteen months fly fishing, writing, and photographing. *Black Empress* is a product of their time in Iran, India, and Nepal.

Bobbi became a professional photographer and copywriter after completing her airline career. From knowledge gained as an employee at Sierra Designs, she started the Angler's Calendar and Catalog Company in 1975. The calendars eventually sold in thirty foreign countries, and in 1993 the business won Exporter of the Year for the State of Idaho, small company category.

Bobbi was a twenty-year member of the Outdoor Writers Association of America, an Arnold Gingrich Writer's recipient from the International Federation of Fly Fishers, and a nine-year board member for The Nature Conservancy in Idaho. She is currently the president of the Authors Guild of Tennessee.

*Black Empress* is the second of four planned world travel books. The first, *Behind the Smile* concerned her days as an international flight attendant during the glamour years of aviation. *Black Empress* describes her time in Iran, India, and Nepal and the rescue of a black Labrador puppy. Her third book, *Home on the Range*, will portray the unusual events of a city girl living on a large ranch in Idaho. The last book will depict her hitchhiking, backpacking, and fly fishing from Africa (climbing Mt. Kilimanjaro) to the United Kingdom, and New Zealand.

I love hearing from readers. Feel free to contact me at my website, and I'll respond directly. Happy reading!

**booksbybobbi.com**

# BLACK EMPRESS

## BOBBI PHELPS WOLVERTON

$_____ $14.95 times _____ number of signed copies.
$_____ 9% Tax ($1.35 each book if mailed to Tennessee).
$_____ U.S.A. Shipping & Handling. ($2.99 each book).

**$_____ Total** ($17.94 each book w/o tax). Ck # _____
Make check out to Village Concepts.

Email: _____

Visa/ MC #: _____

Expiration: _____ 3-Digit Code: _____

Mailing address:
    Street: _____

    City: _____

    State: _____ Zip: _____

Email for multiple order discount. No returns allowed.

## www.booksbybobbi.com
### www.bobbiphelpswolverton.com

Village Concepts, LLC, 124 Chota Shores, Loudon TN 37774.

**Also Available on Amazon.**

# BEHIND THE SMILE

## During the Glamour Years of Aviation

## BOBBI PHELPS WOLVERTON

$_____ $14.95 times _____ number of signed copies.
$_____ 9% Tax ($1.35 each book if mailed to Tennessee).
$_____ U.S.A. Shipping & Handling. ($2.99 each book).

**$_____ Total** ($17.94 each book w/o tax). Ck # _____
Make check out to Village Concepts.

Email: _____

Visa/ MC #: _____

Expiration: _____ 3-Digit Code: _____

Mailing address:
  Street: _____

  City: _____

  State: _____ Zip: _____

Email for multiple order discount. No returns allowed.

## www.booksbybobbi.com

### www.bobbiphelpswolverton.com

Village Concepts, LLC, 124 Chota Shores, Loudon TN 37774.
Also Available on Amazon as an eBook, paperback, and audio.